For Gabby,

from Mike.

Christmas   1944.

THE ENGLISHMAN'S CASTLE

FOUR CENTURIES OF BUILDING AT LUDLOW.

THE
ENGLISHMAN'S
CASTLE

*A history of houses, large and small,
in town and country, from A.D. 100
to the present day*

By

JOHN GLOAG

With drawings by

MARJORY
WHITTINGTON

LONDON
EYRE & SPOTTISWOODE
1944

This book is dedicated to the experts—the officials, the reformers, the architects, the teachers —who make plans for the way their fellow-countrymen should live, in the hope that all such highly-qualified technicians will remember that the Englishman's House is his Castle.

First published 1944

THIS BOOK IS PRODUCED IN COMPLETE
CONFORMITY WITH THE AUTHORIZED
ECONOMY STANDARDS

PRINTED IN GREAT BRITAIN FOR
EYRE AND SPOTTISWOODE (PUBLISHERS) LIMITED
15, BEDFORD STREET, LONDON, W.C.2

CONTENTS

CHAPTER   PAGE

I.   CLIMATE, MATERIALS, BUILDERS AND ARCHITECTS   9

II.   THE HOUSE IN ROMAN BRITAIN (A.D. 100–400)   13

III. THE ANGLO-SAXON HOUSE (A.D. 500–1066)   22

IV.   THE NORMAN-ENGLISH HOME (A.D. 1100–1250)   31

V.   MEDIAEVAL ENGLISH HOMES (A.D. 1250–1450)   41

VI.   EARLY TUDOR HOUSES (A.D. 1450–1558)   51

VII. THE ELIZABETHAN HOME (A.D. 1558–1603)   61

VIII. EARLY STUART HOUSES (A.D. 1603–1640)   73

IX.   THE PURITAN HOME (A.D. 1640–1660)   83

X.   THE GOLDEN AGE OF BUILDING BEGINS (A.D. 1660–1680)   90

XI.   PROGRESS IN HOUSE DESIGN (A.D. 1680–1700)   98

XII. QUEEN ANNE AND EARLY GEORGIAN HOMES (A.D. 1700–
      1750)   107

XIII. LATE EIGHTEENTH-CENTURY HOUSES (A.D. 1750–1800)   119

XIV. THE GOLDEN AGE OF BUILDING ENDS (A.D. 1800–1850)   132

XV.   THE VICTORIAN HOME (A.D. 1850–1900)   144

XVI. THE TWENTIETH-CENTURY ENGLISHMAN'S CASTLE   153

      APPENDIX—SOME NOTES ON BOOKS TO READ   164
               BOOKS REFERRED TO IN THE TEXT   166
               REFERENCES USED FOR ILLUSTRATIONS   170

      INDEX   172

ILLUSTRATIONS

FULL PAGES IN COLOUR

FACING PAGE

FOUR CENTURIES OF BUILDING AT LUDLOW (*Frontispiece*)

NORMAN CASTLE AND SERFS' DWELLINGS 32

MOATED NORMAN CASTLE 40

EARLY TUDOR TOWN HOUSE 50

ELIZABETHAN MANOR HOUSE 64

LONDON STREET, SIXTEENTH CENTURY 72

COUNTRY HOUSE OF THE TYPE DESIGNED BY INIGO JONES 80

LONDON STREET, AFTER THE GREAT FIRE 96

LATE SEVENTEENTH-CENTURY HOUSE IN SMALL COUNTRY TOWN 106

MARKET SQUARE IN COUNTRY TOWN, EARLY EIGHTEENTH CENTURY 112

STREET IN A FASHIONABLE SPA, REGENCY PERIOD 128

SEASIDE TOWN HOUSE, EARLY NINETEENTH CENTURY 136

THE ENGLAND THAT DICKENS DESCRIBED. THE EIGHT BELLS, HATFIELD 144

A WILLIAM MORRIS ROOM 152

COUNTRY HOUSE OF THE TYPE DESIGNED ABOUT 1900–1910 158

1942 HOUSING SCHEME, DESIGNED BY G. A. JELLICOE, F.R.I.B.A. 162

FULL PAGES IN MONOCHROME

PAGE

INTERIOR OF A ROMAN VILLA-HOUSE 20

SAXON CLEARING AND HOUSE 24

INTERIOR OF NORMAN HALL 36

A MEDIAEVAL STREET SCENE 48

EARLY TUDOR INTERIOR 52

MID-SEVENTEENTH-CENTURY INTERIOR 84

LAMPS AND CANDLESTICKS 105

EARLY EIGHTEENTH-CENTURY GRANDFATHER CLOCK 115

LATE EIGHTEENTH-CENTURY INTERIOR 125

FOUR CENTURIES OF HOUSE BUILDING AT DARTMOUTH 135

MID-VICTORIAN INTERIOR 147

HALF PAGES IN MONOCHROME

	PAGE
THE ROMAN ORDERS	15
THE HYPOCAUST	18
A SAXON BED	27
SAXON WINDOWS	29
MEDIAEVAL CHEST	35
OUTDOOR COOKING	45
COTTAGES AT DEREHAM, NORFOLK	54
A TUDOR FARM	55
FARM OUTBUILDINGS	57
A FRIEZE WINDOW	58
EARLY TUDOR FIREPLACE, CHAIR AND CHEST	60
ELIZABETHAN HOUSES AT SHREWSBURY	68
EARLY SEVENTEENTH-CENTURY BED	71
TILE-HUNG HOUSES IN A SMALL SUSSEX TOWN	75
METHODS OF GLAZING	77
THE ROMAN ORDERS	79
HOUSES AT CHIPPING CAMPDEN	82
HOUSE AT FLADBURY, WORCESTERSHIRE	86
COTTAGES AT RICHMOND, YORKSHIRE	88
COTTAGE IN DEVONSHIRE	92
SEVENTEENTH- AND EARLY EIGHTEENTH-CENTURY WINDOWS	99
SUSSEX HOMESTEAD	101
STONE-BUILT COTTAGES ON THE DIGE, ST. IVES	102
BRACKET CLOCK, 1660	104
TIMBER HOUSES IN KENT	109
WALL LANTERN	122
SMOKER'S SET IN STEEL, ABOUT 1790	131
PARK CRESCENT, REGENT'S PARK, BY JOHN NASH	138
ROW OF HOUSES AT CHIPPING CAMPDEN, 1450 TO 1850	142
MODERN COUNTRY HOUSE, IN THE GEORGIAN TRADITION	161

CHAPTER 1

CLIMATE, MATERIALS, BUILDERS AND ARCHITECTS

I T is an old saying that "an Englishman's house is his castle", and the history of the English home underlines its meaning. For seven hundred years that home has been designed to give shelter and privacy. Beginning in Norman days with the provision of retiring rooms for the lord of the castle so that he and his lady could spend some part of their time away from the general life of the great hall, the home has gradually become a place where privacy is guaranteed, and the outside world shut off by the front door and the window curtains.

This liking for privacy is as widespread in England as the love of liberty, and is indeed a practical example of that love; for English liberties are guaranteed by Law, and unless invited by the owner, nobody may enter a private dwelling without a warrant, which can be issued only by a legal process. The front door to-day is as powerful a guard for preserving privacy as the moat, draw-bridge, portcullis and gates of the Norman castle.

The climate has also had a great effect upon our national character and consequently upon our homes. It is a moist, mild climate, freshened by winds from the surrounding seas. During the year there are west winds blowing on half the days, east winds on one-quarter of the days, and winds from north and from south each on one-tenth of the days.[1] The remaining days are calm. It is rare for a fortnight to pass without rain and equally rare for rain to fall steadily, day after day, for the same period. There are no extremes of heat and cold. Charles II once said, in praise of the climate, that "he could be abroad in the air with pleasure, or at least without trouble and inconvenience, ... most days of the year, and ... most hours of the day ..."[2]

Not only the countryman, but the townsman likes to be out of doors. As an open-air man, the Englishman expects his home to give him protection against the weather; not merely the keeping out of rain and wind—any well-built hut could do that—but protection from the character of the weather, so that on a gloomy, damp, foggy day in November or January, he can be cosy, with a good fire for company, while thick walls and well-curtained windows guard his comfort. The dampness of our climate has given us a liking for

---

[1] *Great Britain: Essays in Regional Geography*. Chap. I, "The Climate of Great Britain," by H. R. Mill, pages 8–9.
[2] Recorded by Sir William Temple, 1685.

9

visible heat, and an abundance of coal has enabled every type of English home to indulge that liking.

Plenty of good building materials have allowed sturdy houses to be made, of wood and plaster, stone and brick. There were once great forests of oak, and among the native trees were the ash, alder, birch, willow, yew, hazel, hornbeam, aspen, wych elm and, possibly, the common elm and the beech.[1] A wide belt of limestone runs northwards from Dorset through Somerset and Gloucester, curving north-east through the Midlands to the Yorkshire coast. It has been described, from a building point of view, as "the geological backbone of England".[2] The limestone band has for centuries furnished a material that is easy to quarry, easy to shape and carve, and in the Cotswold country, and throughout its path to Yorkshire, it has allowed builders to make strong, comfortable houses, that look as though they had grown naturally from the ground.

Granite is found in the south-west, in Cornwall and Devon, also in Wales and in the North; sandstone mainly in the Midlands and in Cheshire, Lancashire and West Yorkshire. Granite is hard, enduring, but difficult to work; sandstone is soft, and is sometimes damaged by weather and, in cities, by smoke, but some kinds are good for building.

Clay and chalk are found in the south and east of England. Bricks and tiles are made from clay; and lime, which is one of the ingredients of plaster, is made by burning chalk or limestone.

The way all these materials were used has, in the past, shown how civilisation was growing, flourishing or decaying. In Roman times, the men who used them were often slaves, working under an overseer and carrying out the directions of an architect; sometimes they would be independent craftsmen, handymen who with a few simple tools could build houses with wood, for that is the first material men choose when they want something better than a tent of skins or a basket-work hut of reeds or sticks to shelter them. In the Middle Ages, teams of masons, woodworkers, tilers and other skilled men, would work in partnership, directed by some master-builder. After the sixteenth century, the architect began to take control of house building. At first he was only concerned with very large houses, but in the course of two centuries, he became the master-brain in building, and nearly every type of house was influenced by his ideas.

The architect is a creative controller of building. He has appeared in every civilisation of which we have records; in Egypt, China, India, Assyria, Greece and Rome. A Roman architect, named

[1] *A Pocket-Book of British Trees*, by E. H. B. Boulton.
[2] *Theory and Elements of Architecture*, by Robert Atkinson and Hope Bagenal, Chap. III, page 82.

Marcus Vitruvius Pollio, wrote and published a work on architecture in ten books, during the reign of the emperor Augustus. He had some wise things to say, and his widom still applies. "An architect," he wrote, "should be ingenious, and apt in the acquisition of knowledge. Deficient in either of these qualities, he cannot be a perfect master. He should be a good writer, a skilful draughtsman, versed in geometry and optics, acquainted with history . . ."[1] A modern architect, Howard Robertson, has said: "No layman can realise how many able individuals have to be rolled into one to produce a single *great* architect."[2]

It is the business of an architect to study the building needs of his client, and to meet them by good planning so that the building is fully fit for its purpose and is pleasant in use. In architecture, said Vitruvius, "two considerations must be constantly kept in view; namely, the intention, the matter used to express that intention; but the intention is founded on a conviction that the matter wrought will fully suit the purpose . . ."

Planning is the art of arranging the spaces to be enclosed by the walls of a building, so that they are well-proportioned and comfortably and conveniently related to each other. (Town-planning is a large-scale application of that same art of arrangement, so that the buildings in a town are conveniently placed and related to each other and to the centres of social life.) One of the best and simplest descriptions of the architect's work is given by Howard Robertson in these words: "It is his function to take the client's instructions and prepare the designs which, when approved, the builder will execute. He will advise upon the selection of the builder, and will transmit to the latter in all cases the client's instructions. It is his duty to represent his client's interests as far as the builder is concerned, and at the same time it is his duty to see that the builder is in all ways fairly treated. He is, in fact, an intermediary between the two parties.

"The architect is familiar in general terms with the builder's work. He is acquainted with the general business of each 'trade', such as that of the bricklayer, carpenter, plumber, etc.; indeed, he must have this knowledge to prepare intelligently the working plans, which are accompanied by a complete description of the materials which are to be used and the manner of employing them. This document is called the 'Specification', and it, together with the working drawings, expresses to the builder the conception and details of the design which is to be executed.

"The architect is not superior or even equal to the builder in technical knowledge, but he has a detached and broad view of the

[1] *The Architecture of Marcus Vitruvius Pollio*, translated by Joseph Gwilt (1826), Book I, Chap. I, pp. 3-4.
[2] *Architecture Explained*, by Howard Robertson.

essentials of sound building; and, in addition, he is a specialist in his own field of design, having presumably devoted the major part of his technical education to this subject. It therefore follows that, in this particular field, there is every chance that the architect will be the best qualified person to produce a building having the qualities of good design; in other words, a work of good architecture."[1]

Yesterday, the architect's client was often the nobleman who wanted a town or country house; to-day he may be asked to design a housing scheme for a city or borough council, a block of flats, an office building, a shopping centre, a railway station or a factory. The clients, the building methods and the materials change; but the problem for the architect is the same, and makes the same claim on his skill. Whether he is dealing with bricks and mortar or concrete and steel, he must still design buildings that make the best use of the right materials, use the site on which they stand to the best advantage, and secure the best accommodation for the money that is available. They must also be soundly constructed, fit for their purpose, and pleasant in use.

For seven centuries, the Englishman's castle, large or small, has been changing its shape, its colour and its contents, and, for the last four hundred years, has been gaining new comforts. Compared with men and women of the twelfth and thirteenth centuries, we are unbelievably coddled and protected, with our gas-fires, radiators, electric light, deeply-sprung upholstered chairs and settees, pure drinking water, refrigerators, hot baths, sanitation, drainage, glazed windows, damp-proof walls, vacuum-cleaners and carpeted floors. Only once before had houses in this country approached our modern standards of comfort, and that was when Britain was a Roman province.

The chapters that follow tell the story of the house from that far-off time to the present day. They will deal, period by period, with the large house and the small, in the country and the town; the homes of nobleman and peasant, merchant and artisan—all of them homes, that, as the centuries pass, show, with local variations, the Englishman's devotion to and understanding of the art of living a private life.

[1] *Architecture Explained*, Chap. I, pp. 22–23.

12

CHAPTER II

THE HOUSE IN ROMAN BRITAIN

(A.D. 100–400)

ETWEEN Julius Caesar's first expedition to Britain in B.C. 55 and the Claudian invasion in A.D. 43, the natives of the country had learnt a lot about the nature of Roman civilisation. Trading stations had been established, one on the site of London, luxury goods were imported, and the wine trade with Rome thrived. But although the Britons had allowed traders into the south-eastern parts of their country, they fiercely resisted military conquest.

The Romans found it a hard country to conquer and a dangerous one to hold down. British civilisation had grown and spread along the hills and ridgeways, and villages were built in a few forest clearings, roughly fortified against wolves and unfriendly neighbours. The ways of life varied from tribe to tribe. Immense tracts of forest spread over the country; the rivers turned many valleys into sodden marshes, and such natural barriers kept the native tribes separate, suspicious and often savage. These Celtic tribesmen had made a queer, patchwork civilisation of their own. Sullen and fierce, some of them kept to the forests, and from the beginning to the end of Roman rule, they were untamed and untameable.

Although some of the tribes had a few arts and crafts, they only built the simplest forms of shelter, huts made of basket work, known as "wattle", sometimes daubed with clay, and roofed with turf. They had good potters and metal workers. Their craftsmen had excellent taste. "One of the most striking points about their art is that so often they knew exactly where to stop; for some of their most telling pieces of metal work have only a few bold lines of ornament, yet so arranged as to give the greatest pleasure to the eye. In other words, the Celtic Cymry were artists and craftsmen who did not suffer from that dread of blank space, which so often led to an overloading with unnecessary ornamentation of the work of their Teutonic successors."[1]

These native arts suggest that the ability to build was only awaiting the encouragement that established law and order could give. But when that settled condition came, a ready-made architecture came with it, as efficient in its way as the Roman military machine. Celtic art disappeared for over three-and-a-half centuries.

The Roman came as a conqueror. Military power, law and order,

[1] *The Earlier Inhabitants of London*, by F. G. Parsons, F.R.C.S., F.S.A., Chap. III, p. 96.

advanced north and west over the island, leaving only a few backwaters of savagery in the depths of the forests and on the high moorlands; but coming finally to a stop in Scotland. The Romans walled out the barbaric north; of the two walls they built, one ran from the Firth of Forth to the Firth of Clyde, the Antonine Wall, and the other, Hadrian's Wall, from Solway Firth to Wallsend, near Newcastle. The Antonine Wall was an advanced frontier and was eventually abandoned. It was south of Hadrian's Wall that the province of Britain became a settled part of the Empire.

Roads were made, linking up ports and camps, running like arrows from place to place, providing a network of good-surfaced, safe ways for traffic. "Most of the Roman roads were surveyed . . . in straight sections from skyline to skyline. As a rule the whole course of the road rarely goes more than a mile or so out of a dead straight line, except for quite local deviations round a particularly steep valley or something like that. But where it does alter its course, it does so on a skyline."[1] Where the road passed through forests, the trees and bushes were cleared, so that on either side lay open ground, which afforded no cover for lurking savages. Rivers and streams were bridged, and across fens and marshes the road was carried on a causeway. Camps and trading settlements grew into cities; in the south and west the country became orderly and secure.

The Roman conquest imposed a superior foreign civilisation on the country. In the course of a century or so, that civilisation was accepted by the natives, and Britons became Roman citizens. It is possible that many British chiefs and landowners imitated the habits of the Roman officials who had originally settled in the province, living in comfortable, well-appointed country houses instead of the crude huts of their forefathers. "The Roman villa was the estate of a landowner, and it included not only his own residence, the villa-house, but the farm buildings, labourers' huts and the bailiff's house."[2]

The villa-houses had high standards of comfort. They were heated by a system which kept rooms at an even temperature; they had efficient plumbing, hot and cold water, and baths of generous proportions. Between the Romano-British period, which lasted for nearly four hundred years, and the mid-nineteenth century, these conveniences were not enjoyed by householders.

The Romans had a standardised form of architecture, which had been adapted from Greek models. Although they had made a great architectural invention, the arch, they preferred to go on using forms that had been worked out for what is called post and lintel architecture, a lintel being a horizontal member held up by two vertical posts. Although they had invented the arch, they never

---

[1] *Along the Roman Roads*, by Geoffrey Boumphrey, Chap. I, p. 19.
[2] *Romano-British Buildings and Earthworks*, by John Ward, F.S.A., Chap. VI, p. 156.

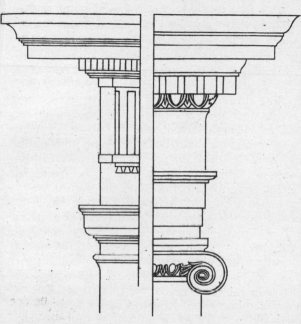

THE ROMAN ORDERS

The Greeks used three orders of architecture: Doric, Ionic
and Corinthian. The Romans added the Tuscan and
Composite orders. They were standardised and used
everywhere in the Roman Empire. Here are three of the
Roman Orders: (1) Tuscan, which is a simplified form
of Doric; (2) Ionic, with spiral volutes on the capitals,
and (3) Corinthian, with capitals of acanthus leaves.

used it inventively, and their buildings remained stiff and formal.
There were set shapes and fixed proportions for everything. Such
features as columns, doorways and mouldings never changed.
Ornament was mass-produced to patterns in much the same way
as goods are mass-produced in a modern factory, the dull repetition work being done by slaves instead of by machines. Any
native ability for carving and decorating was discouraged by this
standardised way of ornamenting everything that had been worked
out centuries before in Italy, and repeated without variation or
imagination all over the provinces of the Empire. Throughout
Europe, North Africa and the Near East, Roman remains display
the same features, the same carved ornament, the same mouldings,
the same lack of new or lively ideas. There were five Roman
"orders": Tuscan, Doric, Ionic, Corinthian and Composite, each
with their special set of columns and capitals, their special types of

moulding, their lines of leafy and geometric ornament. Altars to the gods, triumphal arches to the Emperors, the columns of the forum in every city, the columns that supported the covered way inside the courtyards of houses—all had a rigid sameness.

The only variations came from the use of local building materials. For example, in the Cotswolds, the Romano-British builders used stone; in Hampshire, Sussex, and the Home Counties, they used brick and tile; and, although none of it has survived, they probably used a great deal of timber. How they used these materials, and how they planned the villas they built, was laid down for them by Roman architects, who followed long-established and unalterable rules and regulations. In the sixth of his ten books on architecture, Vitruvius has chapters describing in great detail "the forms of houses suited to different ranks of persons", and the way in which different parts of the house are to be designed. Chapter IX deals with "the proportions of houses in the country". It is full of practical wisdom, carefully recorded, but it leaves little to the imagination. The size of such houses "should be dependent on the extent of the land attached to them, and its produce. The courts and their dimensions will be determined by the number of cattle, and the yokes of oxen employed. . . . The baths should be contiguous to the kitchen, for they will then be serviceable also for agricultural purposes. . . . If villas are required to be erected of more magnificence than ordinary, they must be formed according to the proportions laid down for town houses . . . but with the precautions necessary to prevent the purposes of a country house being interfered with."[1]

The country house was often of the corridor type, with a courtyard enclosed on three sides by a covered corridor which shaded and protected the ground-floor rooms. The ground-floor was of brick and tile, or stone, and the upper floor of wood, with a tiled or possibly a thatched roof. There were windows, with small panes of glass, set in wood or metal frames.[2] This glass was obscure, seldom less than one-eighth of an inch thick, and of greenish-blue colour.[3] The walls of the rooms were generally plastered, and painted in lively colours with a variety of decorative subjects: birds, flowers, nymphs and fauns, arranged in orderly panels, with a dado below, sometimes painted to imitate marble.

In the principal rooms, a mosaic pavement would be found. This stone carpet might be of simple, geometrical design; but many pavements were elaborate, with figures of gods and strange, mythical monsters—clearly the work of highly skilled men—and their

[1] *Vitruvius*, Book VI, Chap. IX, pp. 181–182.
[2] *Londinium*, by W. R. Lethaby, Chap. I, p. 31. Also *Reading Museum Guide to the Silchester Collection*, by Mill Stephenson, F.S.A., p. 20.
[3] *Romano-British Buildings and Earthworks*, by John Ward, Chap. XI, p. 271.

colouring must have given an air of warmth and comfort to a room. "The daily life of the richer sections of the Romano-British community was passed amid surroundings in which colour played a considerable part, and to appreciate this we have only to think of the brilliant polychrome appearance of many mosaics, of the elaborately painted walls, the wide range of colours in the finer ceramic wares, the sumptuous mottled glasses, and the fine enamels."[1]

The house would be comfortably furnished, with beds, tables, stools, chairs and couches. Most of this furniture would be made of wood, and some chairs possibly of wicker. Often the legs of chairs and tables would be formed like the legs of animals, ending in claws or hooves. Roman furniture in metal has survived in other countries, and on the sites of Romano-British houses thousands of household objects in bronze and iron have been found, from nutcrackers to candlesticks, cooking utensils and all kinds of tools. The house would be equipped with vessels of pottery and glass, and in the Silchester collection there are "bottles, one or two-handled, to hold liquor, large wide-mouthed jars for storage of dry foodstuffs, smaller ones with rims for fixing coverings, probably for preserving comestibles in oil or pickle, kitchen pans, and other forms, all intended for domestic use."[2] There was a great variety of pottery, and dishes and vessels of pewter were also in use. Drinking cups were sometimes cheerfully inscribed. One of those in the Silchester collection reads: VITAM TIBI, "Long life to thee".

Kitchens were well equipped; there were brick or stone built ovens, and charcoal was probably used for cooking.

Floors and walls were heated by means of a hypocaust. Below the centre of the floor there was a chamber, two or three feet high, with rows of brick pillars set close together to support the floor. From this shallow chamber ducts ran under the floor to the walls and were carried up through them by means of hollow box tiles, built in with the masonry, and emerging at the eaves of the house. One of the ducts came through the wall of the building direct from the chamber to the outside, where there was a stoke hole. This duct became a furnace and lighted fuel was pushed into it so that the heat passed to the underground chamber and ascended through the ducts in the walls. The tops of these ducts, when they reached the eaves, may have been sheltered with small chimney pots, or some form of capping or hood in brick, stone or plaster, to prevent rain from dribbling down them. During winter a Roman house must have had little quivering threads of smoke ascending all along the tops of the outside walls. Inside the room there was no visible heating apparatus at all.

---

[1] *Anglo-Saxon Art*, by T. D. Kendrick, F.S.A., Chap. II, p. 39.
[2] *Reading Museum Guide to the Silchester Collection*, p. 31.

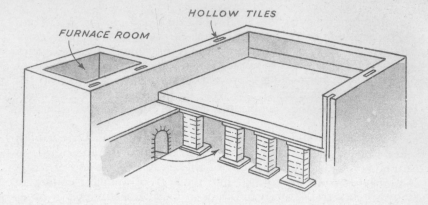

FURNACE ROOM

HOLLOW TILES

THE HYPOCAUST

Diagram of a room in a Roman house, showing the shallow chamber below
the floor and the hollow tiles in the wall used in the heating system.

The houses themselves were spacious and inviting. With their
timber-framed upper storeys and thatched or tiled roofs, they were
probably not unlike Elizabethan English houses. Courses of brick
and tile, in the brick-using parts of the country, would be bound
with an iron-hard mortar. "Roman builders early learned how to
make good mortar and concrete, being careful to use clean coarse
gravel and finely-divided lime. They also found that an addition of
crushed tiles and pottery was an improvement and, for their good
work, used so much of this that the mortar became quite red."[1]

The Romano-British landowner had a well-planned and even
luxurious country house, lit by night with lamps and candles. He
would number among his possessions an assortment of decorative
objects in bronze, glass, pottery and stone; pieces of sculpture;
curtains and cushions in rich, imported fabrics. He also enjoyed that
great, old-world labour-saving device—a large staff of servants.
His land was cultivated by his slaves and he may have let some of
it out to semi-independent peasants who were half-way to being
serfs. "The peasantry who worked on these estates or were other-
wise occupied in the country, lived in rude hamlets, sometimes in pit
dwellings, sometimes in houses, with few circumstances of comfort
or pleasure."[2] The slave quarters would seldom be more than wattle-
and-daub huts.

An imaginative picture of the sort of life that was lived by Roman
landowners in peaceful South Britain, is given in Kipling's stories

[1] *Londinium*, by W. R. Lethaby, Chap. I, p. 12.
[2] *Victoria County History, Hampshire* (F. Haverfield), I, pp. 269–270.

about the young Centurion of the Thirtieth Legion, in *Puck of Pook's Hill*. The placid course of that life is contrasted in those stories with the vivid excitement of a visit to some brilliant little city like Aquae Sulis, as Bath was then called. The Roman cities were well laid out, and we know exactly how many of them were arranged. Between the two world wars, air surveys have disclosed the bones of many forgotten towns and settlements—for the lines of ancient streets are still marked by different coloration in the growth of grass and crops, and by faint ridges and depressions, invisible at ground level, which still hold their lines of shadow in our slanting sunlight when viewed from above. Some towns vanished for ever, like Silchester (Calleva Atrebatum) in Hampshire, and Viroconium in Shropshire. Some cities remained for hundreds of years in ruins after Roman law and order were mere memories. Gerald de Barri—Giraldus Cambrensis—travelled through Wales in the twelfth century and visited what had once been the Roman city of Caerleon. He described its remains in some detail. "This city," he said, "was of undoubted antiquity, and handsomely built of masonry, with courses of bricks, by the Romans. Many vestiges of its former splendour may yet be seen; immense palaces, formerly ornamented with gilded roofs, in imitation of Roman magnificence, inasmuch as they were first raised by the Roman princes, and embellished with splendid buildings; a tower of prodigious size, remarkable hot baths, relics of temples, and theatres, all inclosed within fine walls, parts of which remain standing. You will find on all sides, both within and without the circuit of the walls, subterraneous buildings, aqueducts, underground passages; and what I think worthy of notice, stoves contrived with wonderful art, to transmit the heat insensibly through narrow tubes passing up the side walls."[1]

Caerleon carried a strong mark of its Roman personality through the Middle Ages, the Reformation, and rise of the British Empire —right down to the nineteenth century. Arthur Machen, who was born there, recalls that, when he was a boy, there was an odd New Year's Day celebration in the town. The children would get a big apple and put bits of gold leaf on it and stick raisins in it. They also stuck in little sprigs of box and slit the ends of hazel nuts and put them on to the ends of the box leaves. Three bits of stick were fixed into the base of the apple, and it was then carried, on this tripod, round from house to house, and the children were given cakes and sweets by the householders. Arthur Machen identifies this as the ancient custom of the *strena*. He says: ". . . nobody knew what it was all about. And here is the strangeness of it. Caerleon means the fort of the legions, and for about three hundred years the

---

[1] *The Itinerary through Wales, etc.*, by Giraldus Cambrensis, Chap. V, pp. 50–51.

INTERIOR OF A ROMAN VILLA-HOUSE

These houses with their courtyards, corridors, luxurious plumbing and central heating, had no influence at all on the subsequent development of architecture in England.

Second Augustan Legion was quartered there, and made a tiny Rome of the place, with amphitheatre, baths, temples, and everything necessary for the comfort of a Roman-Briton. And the Legion brought over the custom of the *strena* (French, *etrennes*), the New Year's gift of good omen. The apple, with its gold leaf, raisins and nuts meant: 'good crops and wealth in the New Year' . . . and I suppose that Caerleon was the only place south of the Tweed where people took any festal notice at all of the first day in the year. For it is not an old English festival at all. It is distinctly Latin in origin."[1]

The towns had a busy and agreeable life of their own. Professor Lethaby has suggested that "Londinium was a little Alexandria in the West and represented Britain as the other did Egypt. The building of such a city called together many able craftsmen—builders sculptors, painters and mosaic workers. There must also have been shipbuilders and a due proportion of craftsmen-producers, potters, bone-and-metal-workers, shoemakers, clothiers and the rest."[2] The streets were paved and clean; the houses had a water supply and a drainage system. The public buildings had a stiff but impressive dignity.

The town houses of officials and well-to-do merchants would have all the features of a country house, but they would be without bathrooms. Each town had its own public baths; they were centres of social intercourse and a visit to these luxurious establishments was part of the day's routine. Even a small place like Silchester had the most beautifully appointed baths. The cities had not only their baths; they had amphitheatres for games.

The artisans and slaves would live in blocks of houses, and these would be erected to an architect's plan, and run up fairly cheaply in brick, sometimes three or even four storeys in height.

The bones of these old Romano-British cities lie beneath the modern streets and buildings of London, York, Lincoln, Chester, Bath, Gloucester, Cirencester, and many other places that still live. But our period as a Roman province left no mark upon the architecture of the country; it had no influence on the form or character of the English house. Although the province of Britain endured for nearly four centuries, by the time the Normans arrived in England the only material traces of Roman rule were a few ruins, a fine system of roads, and possibly two additions to our native stock of trees— the sweet chestnut and the black poplar.

[1] The essay entitled "Why New Year?" in *Dog and Duck*, by Arthur Machen.
[2] *Londinium*, by W. R. Lethaby, Chap. X, p. 194.

CHAPTER III

THE ANGLO-SAXON HOUSE
(A.D. 500–1066)

DURING the fifth century Britain ceased to be a Roman province. Early in that century, the last Imperial troops were withdrawn for service on the Continent, and although the official machinery of government may have limped along for a while, year after year the barbarians drove farther into the country, Picts coming from the North, through the broken and deserted Wall, and Saxons from the South and East coasts. What remained of Romano-British civilisation was pushed farther and farther westwards. The Romanised Celtic tribes, badly led and quarrelling among themselves, fought a long, losing battle. Wales was the last stronghold of those who stayed in the Island, but many Britons migrated to France, and the land where they found refuge is still called Brittany.

As the province was gradually overrun by the barbarians who were our ancestors, the nature of town and country life changed. There are few records of what happened in the two hundred years that lie between the end of the fourth century and the landing of St. Augustine's mission in 597; but there are plenty of legends. It seems likely that the Celtic tribesmen were at last rallied by some powerful leader; though the figure we know as King Arthur, may well have been an overworked Roman officer, a gifted general who delayed the westward drive of the barbarian invasions. In this long war against an enemy who was constantly strengthened by land-hungry reinforcements from Northern Europe, civilisation was trampled under-foot. The Saxon conquerors were after loot and land. Grass and field flowers soon covered the ruins they made. After they had taken and looted a town, they ignored it: they seemed to avoid all the old places of settlement, perhaps with super-stitious dislike. They made their own clearings, defended them with ditches and stockades, and built crude, timber-framed houses and halls, with thatched or turfed roofs, and wattle-and-daub walls. Many of the arts and crafts of building were lost. Although ruined Roman houses must have continually reminded the Saxons of vanished skill, the desire to build had gone. Writing of this dark age, Mr. T. D. Kendrick draws a bleak picture of desolation: "For with architecture went much else, and as the buildings crumbled, so the statues fell, the memorials were broken and neglected, the paintings peeled off the house-walls, and the weeds grew where the pavements had been. And nothing took their place; not indeed until the days of

Paulinus and of Benedict Biscop in the seventh century. Over two hundred years for the beggarly Saxon world of wooden halls to scorn, to destroy, and to forget that impressive stamp of Roman greatness that had been laid so laboriously upon this far-off province of Britain."[1]

A few elementary crafts remained, but it was not until two centuries after the wars and invasions that ended the Roman province that building was again practised with skill, and materials other than timber were used.[2] Britain was no longer a united country; it became, and remained for some centuries, a collection of warring, barbaric states. Christian missions spread artistic ideas, and some states, in particular Northumbria, enjoyed a period of comparative security, in which architecture revived. (A church built on the Isle of Lindisfarne in 652 was made of hewn oak and covered with reeds, but Bishop Eadbert removed the thatch and covered both walls and roof with lead plates.)[3] The Venerable Bede, in his history, refers to "the peaceable and calm disposition of the times."[4] He was writing of the year 731.

The Anglo-Saxon states had made a civilisation of their own. Slowly town life revived. In the seventh century, London was a trading port, where merchants lived and had offices and warehouses. But town and country never enjoyed a really long period of peace. In the middle of the ninth century, London was sacked by the Vikings, and between 994 and 1016 the city was three times beseiged by raiders. But the raiders who stayed to become settlers during the six centuries that lay between the Roman province and the Norman conquest were not ignorant of skilled crafts, although they did not at first apply them to building.

All those raiding races depended greatly upon the skill of ship-wrights, and up and down the northern coasts of Europe inventions were constantly being made in the art of ship-building. In time, the skill thus acquired by wood-workers was reflected in building. In Norway, for example, a remarkable and beautiful architecture of wood grew up; in England, wood-workers profited generation after generation by the slow spread of ideas that had been tried out in the course of ship-building and which taught builders new ways of using timber in houses and churches, particularly in roofs. Towards the end of the Anglo-Saxon period, great skill in wood-working existed in England, and it arose from a partnership between forester, shipwright and builder; their knowledge was pooled, their skills were interchangeable.

In the Saga of King Olaf Trygvesson, there is an account of the

[1] *Anglo-Saxon Art*, by T. D. Kendrick, F.S.A., Chap. III, p. 47.
[2] *Ibid.*, Chap. VI, p. 111.
[3] *Bede's Ecclesiastical History*, Book III, Chap. XXV.
[4] *Ibid.*, Book V, Chap. XXIII.

SAXON CLEARING AND HOUSE

Often the Saxon house would take the form of a wooden tower built on some eminence, surrounded by a stockade. Outside that fortified area, the wattle-and-daub, thatched huts of the villagers would be grouped.

24

building of a ship called *Long Serpent*. The master-shipwright was Thorberg Skafhogg, and he invented an early form of streamlining. When the carpenters were planking the ship, the king inspected it, and discovered that "somebody had gone from stem to stern, and cut one deep notch after the other down the one side of the planking."[1] The king was dismayed, until Thorberg chipped the planks so that the deep notches were all smoothed away, which vastly improved the shape of the vessel.

This happens to be recorded, but hundreds of unrecorded ways of shaping wood, new methods of jointing, and new associations of wood with other materials, must have been thought of, century after century, by men who did most of their thinking with their hands, and whose skill we can appreciate to-day from the evidence provided by the woodwork and stonework of mediaeval churches, palaces and guildhalls. All this skill began with the making of houses for the rovers who, every few generations, assaulted the security of the country, conquered some land, and settled on it to farm and to found families. Occasionally some enlightened Saxon noble may have repaired and used a Roman country house: illustrations in ninth and tenth century manuscripts suggest that these houses still existed and that they were occasionally occupied, though such evidence is unreliable. "Not a single villa in the country has been found underlying a Saxon dwelling or has yielded evidence of permanent occupation in the Saxon period."[2]

Generally the country house was a hall, a large, timber-framed building, thatched, vulnerable to fire, and blackened inside by smoke from open hearths. That smoke escaped through a hole in the roof. The size of these crude chimneys may be gauged by a reference in the Saga of King Olaf Trygvesson. The king had invited some sorcerers to a party, with the intention of killing them, for practising witchcraft. He allowed them all to be seated in one room, "which was well adorned", provided a feast, and made them drunk. He then ordered the house to be set on fire. Only one man escaped, and he climbed through the smoke-hole in the roof.[3] Not only would such a large opening let smoke out, it would also let rain and snow in, though it is possible that some kind of shield was fixed above the hole.

The great hall sheltered a form of communal life that would have horrified a Romano-British landowner by its lack of privacy, its crudity, its dirt and general discomfort. The Saxon tolerated draughts, vermin, rainwater, wood smoke, sputtering torches

[1] *Heimskringla: The Olaf Sagas*, by Snorre Sturlason. King Olaf Trygvesson's Saga, Chap. XCV, p. 77.
[2] *Roman Britain and the English Settlements*, by R. G. Collingwood and J. N. L. Myres. XIX, "Britain in the Fifth Century". pp. 317-318.
[3] *Heimskringla: The Olaf Sagas*, by Snorre Sturlason. King Olaf Trygvesson's Saga, Chap. LXIX, "The Burning of the Warlocks."

dipped in fat in place of candles and lamps at night, clumsy furniture, roughly hewn from blocks of wood, beds built against a wall and closed in at night with shutters; he had no drainage, no baths; no water supply apart from wells—in fact, he displayed an ignorant disregard for the refinements of life, an ignorance which the Roman citizen had always associated with the barbarians who lived beyond the frontiers of the Empire. Even the highest standards of such barbaric life were far below those of Roman Britain. In the Saga of Saint Olaf, there are some references to the furnishing of a room. When King Olaf was about to visit his step-father, King Sigurd, there was much energetic preparation for his arrival. The servants were ordered to bring out hangings and benches. "Two carles brought straw for the floor, two brought forward four-cornered tables and the drinking jugs . . ."[1] Jugs, for swilling down ale. Elegantly served meals, good wines, polite conversation, deliberations and discussions about literature and music: all these belonged to a half-forgotten golden age, to a culture that had faded into an almost mythical past.

Decoration was lavished upon impermanent things. Even as early as the seventh century, England was famous for embroidery. Occasionally, such rich and elaborate work may have given a touch of luxury to a hall; and it is reported that in the tenth century, a lady of Ely was at some pains to embroider a curtain with scenes illustrating the exploits of her husband.[2]

Apart from churches and monasteries, all building had to take account of the unsettled state of the country and although perhaps many years might pass without a district suffering from raids and warfare, the threat was always present, just over the next range of hills, or beyond the belt of forest. Even churches were not safe from pagan raiders. Towns were walled, great halls were protected by stockades, and in the ninth and tenth centuries the forerunner of the fortified castle appeared, often consisting of a single square tower of wood, perched on some hill and surrounded by a wall composed of turf and wooden stakes. It was an architecture of fear. But although Anglo-Saxon civilisation did not produce either good country or town houses, a few buildings put up at the end of the period, such as St. Alban's Abbey and some small churches, like the one at Bradford-on-Avon in Wiltshire, remain to suggest what might have been done if that civilisation had enjoyed the same standards of security as the Roman province.

The fact that nearly all the domestic building was in timber, which has perished, deprives us of any specimens dating from those troubled centuries; but certain methods of building were worked out and

[1] *Heimskringla: The Olaf Sagas*, by Snorre Sturlason. Saint Olaf's Saga, Chap. XXX, "Aasta's Preparations to receive her son, Olaf."
[2] *English Art in the Middle Ages*, by O. Elfrida Saunders, Chap. V, p. 65.

A SAXON BED

Such beds were like bunks, built along the wall and closed by shutters, which could be fastened on the inside at night, or by curtains.

perfected, and they have endured. The making of bricks had probably ceased and although bricks were used by the builders of St. Alban's Abbey, they were taken from the nearby ruined Roman city of Verulamium, and arranged in the great square tower of the Abbey. The arch was not forgotten, and brick and stone arches with rounded and triangular heads are found in the few buildings that survive from this period; but a new form of arch had been discovered in building with timber.

This arched form of timber framing arose from a partnership between the forester and the builder, possibly with help from the shipwright. The enormous forests of oak trees, which still spread over the land, provided such a variety of growth, that it was an easy task to find timber that would do some of the builder's work for him. It was possible to choose an oak tree that was bent naturally in such a way that, when it was used in a building, part of it would be upright and part would slope, so one-half of a pointed arch could be set up and a similar piece of timber set up opposite, and the two joined at the top, to support the roof ridge. A series of such pieces of timber would be selected, so that the framework of a house looked rather as though a boat was being built upside-down, the keel being the ridge of the roof, and the ribs being the uprights and roof supports. (The word "keel" is still applied to the form of pointed arch known as an ogee.) These parts of the framework were called "crucks", and this form of frame building developed in the Midlands and the North.[1] Actually, the word "cruck" was used in Germany to describe the ribs of boats.

Many country houses, and possibly some of the better houses in a village, would be built on this pointed arch system of timber construction, and sometimes the roof would rest directly on the ground. A well-known example of such building is the house at Scrivelsby, Lincolnshire, called "Teapot Hall", and it consists of one large living room with a bedroom above. It is described locally as:

Teapot Hall,
All roof, no wall.[2]

This system of building on crucks lasted for hundreds of years, and to-day the outlines of the main crucks can often be seen at the end of a half-timbered cottage. From this system came an architecture of wood, which produced many beautiful roofs. As carpenters and builders grew more skilful, they gained greater control over their materials, and gradually new forms and methods were invented, and a store of knowledge was built up, generation by generation, concerning how much weight and strain timber beams and supports could stand. The invention of the cruck system of building was important, because, before that, the roof had to be supported on many wooden uprights; but directly the roof could be supported on an arch of timber that sprang from the walls on each side, then the central floor space was tidied up and cleared of obstructions. Thus the living space of the house grew, and the hall became the great hall.

The life that was sheltered by those great halls was crude and violent. The Saxons, Jutes, Angles and Danes lived for fighting, loot, drinking and gluttony. They had codes and laws of their own, but they easily sank back into savagery. Their contribution to the civilisation of later ages was their seacraft. Their adventurousness opened up new trading routes; their sea roving improved shipbuilding. A vivid picture of the fierce life they lived is given in Eric Linklater's story, *The Men of Ness*. A Jutish chief's household in Sussex is described in Kipling's tale, "The Conversion of St. Wilfrid", in *Rewards and Fairies*. In the Olaf Sagas there are many brief descriptions of country life and buildings, some of which have already been quoted.

Apart from the great halls, only the simplest of shelters were provided for farm-hands. Some of the small farmers may have owned sturdy, timber-framed houses; but the small house usually sheltered animals as well as men, women and children.

[1] This distribution of buildings on crucks is suggested in *The Development of English Building Construction*, by C. F. Innocent, Chap. IV, pp. 35–36.
[2] *The Development of English Building Construction*, by C. F. Innocent, pp. 26–27. Also illustrated with plans and fully described in *The Evolution of the English House*, by S. O. Addy (Revised Edition, 1933), Chap. II, pp. 41–45; and in Nathaniel Lloyd's *A History of the English House*, pp. 11–13, where the descriptive verse is quoted.

SAXON WINDOWS

Windows in the few stone buildings that existed, were small and mean. In wooden buildings they would be mere slits.

In the towns timber buildings would be the rule; though perhaps the shells of a few houses of brick and tile, bound in the iron grip of Roman mortar, would have survived for three or four hundred years. It has been suggested that even as late as King Alfred's time, London was still largely a Roman city in appearance, with its ancient streets maintained by the English population. "Here a Roman mansion, with its mosaic floors, would still be inhabited. There a portico would be patched with gathered bricks and covered with shingles, while by its side stood a house of wattle and daub."[1]

In the Assise of Buildings of 1212, it is said that "in ancient times the greater part of the city was built of wood, and the houses were covered with straw and stubble and the like."[2] Any city with streets of timber houses would be in constant danger from fire, and London has had ten great fires, the first in 961 and the last in 1940. A disastrous fire in 982 probably swept away all traces of Roman buildings that had survived. The machinery of a well-run Roman city had vanished long before; drains, water supply, public baths, efficient heating in houses—such things were not even memories in Anglo-Saxon London. In houses with floors of stone or rammed earth, straw and rushes helped to disperse the chill of rooms, and also gathered dirt and vermin. Even the town house of the well-to-do merchant was by Roman or modern standards a poor, draughty, uncomfortable place. Windows were unglazed; glass was a forgotten luxury, and although a little was used in churches, it was imported from France. Sometimes a window would be filled with panes of horn, but usually those narrow slits in the wall would be

[1] *London Before the Conquest*, by W. R. Lethaby, Chap. VII, p. 157.
[2] Quoted by Lethaby in *London Before the Conquest*, p. 158.

left open to admit daylight, and closed at night with wooden shutters. Rooms were heated by fires on open hearths of stone, or plates of iron; but the smoke was not coaxed through flues and chimneys; as in the great country halls it found its way out through openings in the roof. Cooking was done by means of open fires, though bakers had ovens. Candles were rare; so were oil lamps, and torches dipped in oil or fat and placed in iron sockets fixed into the wall, provided the light in large rooms. For furniture, apart from shut-beds and independent beds, there were tables and stools and benches, possibly some chests. Sometimes this furniture was roughly carved, but the skill of Anglo-Saxon craftsmen was lavished on metal-work, pottery and stone carving. Much of that work displayed by its overcrowded ornament the "dread of blank space".

Nothing survived from the six centuries of turmoil that came before the Norman conquest except a tradition of skill in wood-working, and a few inventions in construction which made good house-building possible.

CHAPTER IV

THE NORMAN-ENGLISH HOME
(A.D. 1100–1250)

BEFORE the Norman Conquest, England, for a short time united under one monarchy, had been in contact with Norman civilisation, just as Britain before the Roman Conquest had been in contact with Rome. The Normans were a talented people. They were good soldiers, good rulers, good builders, and they had acquired standards of living that were quite unknown to the slow, rather indolent Anglo-Saxons. England had grown secure and placid after the Danish invasions.

The Normans, like the Romans, found the country difficult to hold down when once it was conquered, but England was easier to take over than pre Roman Britain because it was united. For some years the country was held by force and the visible symbol of the ruling power was the castle, which was at first a purely military station consisting of the keep, an impregnable tower. From that tower, stark, ruthless and efficient in its building and purpose, the English country house originated. The house grew gradually, and for some centuries it grew behind thick walls, always with the fear of attack as the chief purpose at the back of the builder's mind; but the solitary tower soon became a castle with the keep as the military core, the final stronghold which could withstand a very long siege.

As time went by, and military needs became less pressing, the castle was elaborated. Walls enclosed more and more ground. Beyond the high main walls a curtain wall would often be built, to check raiding forces and to delay attacking armies at the beginning of a siege. If the curtain wall was impossible to hold, then the defending force would retire to the main wall. Unless the castle was built on the crown of a hill, like Corfe in Dorset, the main wall was usually surrounded by a moat. A drawbridge, which could be raised in front of the gateway, crossed the moat. The gate behind that drawbridge was protected by an iron grille, called a portcullis, which descended from the tower above the gateway. Sometimes a tower would also protect the far side of the drawbridge, so that a delaying action could be fought, and the attacking forces engaged in besieging this solitary tower before they could tackle the problem of crossing the moat and scaling the walls beyond it or battering down the gate.

Inside the main walls would be the keep, generally four storeys in height, and in the early Norman castles this contained the great hall, the chapel, kitchens, storehouses and armoury. Far below the ground level were cellars and dungeons. Spiral stairways, built in the thickness of the walls, ascended to the upper floors and the flat roof with its protecting battlements. A castle provisioned for a long siege would be a little, self-supporting city.

Beyond the curtain wall, a street of cottages would accommodate the villagers and dependents of the feudal lord. Their dwellings would hardly differ from those used by Roman slaves and Saxon serfs: they were crude cottages of wattle-and-daub and thatch, some built on crucks. Every time the castle was besieged those cottages would be burned to the ground and their inhabitants taken inside the castle, which they would help to defend until the siege was raised.

The castle was built of stone, and if local material was not available, imported stone would be used. Much of it was shipped across the Channel from Caen in Normandy. The outer walls would be immensely thick; behind them the castle gradually changed its character, and acquired the likeness of a large, rambling, fortified house. The great hall was the centre of life; and it was as communal as the life of a Saxon hall. Even when it occupied the main floor of the keep, the Norman hall was lofty. Additions were made to it from time to time: one or two chambers would bud off, to give extra accommodation, and to allow privileged people to enjoy a little private life. In some keeps a withdrawing room or "solar" would take up part of the floor above the hall.

A fire on a central hearth gave limited warmth to the great hall, but early in the twelfth century the fire was moved to the wall, the hearth was put into a recess, and the smoke carried up through the thickness of the wall. The fireplace had arrived. An early example of such a fireplace is found at Castle Hedingham, in Essex, where the flue that led the smoke from the fire only rose through the wall for a few feet, and let it out through a hole. There was no chimney-stack, no attempt to cope with the effect of a high wind on the fire, which must have blown the smoke back through the hole, out of the fireplace, and into the hall.[1]

At the end of the hall, a raised platform called a däis, would accommodate the tables, stools and benches used by the lord of the castle, his wife, their relatives and guests. It was the privileged part of the great hall; a first step towards privacy.

Drainage and sanitation in the castle were primitive. Latrines, privy chambers or garderobes, were built into the thickness of the wall, and they drained into a pit, and sometimes into the moat of the castle. "Wherever there was a stream running through the moat, it was customary to divert a portion of it and make it flow through the garderobe pit . . ."[2] Examples of garderobes can be seen in the

[1] *A History of the English House*, by Nathaniel Lloyd, Figs. 579 and 580, pp. 352–353.
[2] *Sanitation, An Historical Survey*, by H. A. J. Lamb, A.R.I.B.A., *The Architect's Journal*, Vol. 85, No. 2198, March 4th, 1937, p. 387.

NORMAN CASTLE WITH SERFS' DWELLINGS.

Tower of London, and "at Langley Castle, in Northumberland, no less than four of these apartments were provided for each floor, each one with a separate outlet, discharging into a stream."[1]

Baths were occasionally used, and large tubs were filled with warm water for this purpose, but the habit of bathing was restricted to the higher ranks of society. There were few facilities for personal cleanliness, although clothes and bed linen were frequently washed.

In the years immediately following the Norman Conquest, when military necessity still controlled the form of building, the castle walls would be bare inside, and everything subordinated to the needs of warfare. But, as the country grew quieter, and Saxon opposition was stamped out, the interior of the castle became less bleak. The stone walls were hung with great woven tapestries, depicting hunting scenes, military achievements, and a variety of religious subjects. The round-headed windows were closed at night by wooden shutters: occasionally "a piece of waxed or greased stuff did the work of glass."[2] The chill of the stone-paved floor would be reduced by strewing rushes and straw.

The furniture used would be simple in form, and made by local craftsmen. The castle would probably have a staff of carpenters, whose time was spent upon the maintenance of wood-work in roofs, and who would lend a hand with the rebuilding of the villagers' cottages, when fire or raids had destroyed them. These men would make tables, benches and chests. The simplest form of chest would be hollowed out of a large piece of timber, and these "dug-out" chests were probably in general use, though wood-workers had the skill to construct other types. They would shape and join the sides, but it was a smith's work to bind the timber of a chest with iron and to fit the hinges and locks. Iron bands were only used when objects of value were to be stored in a chest. The smith was the most important craftsman, for he was the armourer, the man who made and repaired weapons.

Beds had quilts, sheets, counterpanes, bolsters and pillows. Fur rugs were used in the richer households. A wooden bedstead was used, though beds were often made directly on the floor of the hall. Host, hostesses and visitors would often sleep in one room. It was not usual to change into night clothes: most people went to bed naked.[3]

The Crusades had a lasting influence on the surroundings of the Norman household. Thousands of pious and adventurous noblemen

[1] *Sanitation Through the Ages*, by Desmond Eyles. *The Official Architect*, Vol. 4, No. 4, April 1941, "The Middle Ages", p. 165.

[2] *Mediaeval England*, 1066–1350, by Mary Bateson, Part II, "The Lawyer's Feudalism", (1154–1250), p. 152.

[3] *A History of Domestic Manners and Sentiments in England*, by Thomas Wright, Chap. XII. Alexander Neckham, writing in the early thirteenth century, describes beds and bedding in great detail, and is quoted by Thomas Wright.

and their followers who became Crusaders, saw the luxurious civilisation of the Eastern Roman Empire. In Constantinople, there were baths and perfumes, rich fabrics, mosaics, glass vessels and ornaments, carvings of rare woods and ivory, intricate metal-work—a host of elaborate and decorative trifles which gave a touch of elegance to life which had been unknown in Western Europe, and particularly in England, for more than six centuries. The Crusaders also learned something about the arts of their enemies, the Saracens, against whom they fought in Palestine. They discovered that the Saracens were not just barbaric infidels; they had inherited all the splendours of Arabian civilisation. They had continued the arts and crafts of the old Roman provinces of Syria and Egypt, and in Spain Arab learning flourished at the great university of Cordova. So when the Crusaders returned, they introduced many foreign ideas into England, and a new, strange abundance of colour began to enliven buildings of all kinds.

The interior of the Romano-British house had been bright with colour; even in Saxon times, a little wall decoration had developed in churches[1]; but when at last Norman-English civilisation became secure, and law and order were established, then colour became an accepted part of life. It seemed as though the Crusaders had brought back with them some of the intense light and vivid glitter of the East. English craftsmen painted and carved in wood and stone; the geometric patterns of the East looped and zig-zagged their way across arches, round columns, and along mouldings; woven fabrics draped walls and screened doorways. Both inside and outside, buildings acquired rich hues. In the towns, gilded spires arose, and the houses that lined the streets began to glow here and there with colour. The Norman period was becoming Norman-English.

No period of building has ever been absolutely complete: periods merge into each other. As we have seen, the Norman period really began when there was still a Saxon king ruling England, and Norman masons had come over before the Conquest and had begun to teach the Saxon-English new ways of building. The purely Norman period of building lasted until the end of the twelfth century. By the thirteenth century, not only were ideas about building changing and improving, but the Norman and Saxon sections of the population were beginning to mix. There is a verse in *Ivanhoe*, Sir Walter Scott's romance of Richard I's time, which is recited by Wamba, a Saxon jester:

> "Norman saw on English oak;
> On English neck a Norman yoke;
> Norman spoon in English dish,
> And England ruled as Normans wish . . ."

[1] *A History of English Art in the Middle Ages*, by O. Elfrida Saunders, Chap. II, p. 29.

MEDIAEVAL CHEST

A "dug-out" chest, made from a single piece of timber, hollowed
out, and fitted with a lid. The form of such chests is conjectural;
but it is likely that the smith would be called in to provide hinges,
strong locks, and sometimes iron bands for the outside.

But the Norman spoon certainly stirred together the best that
was in Saxon and Norman, and architecture, which always reflects
the standards of any civilisation and shows what manner of men
and women made it, begins in the thirteenth century to grow in all
sorts of new ways. A new period of architecture known as Early
English, replaced the massive, simple outlines of Norman building.
The castle still frowned on the countryside; but within the castle,
the chapel and the great hall and the rooms that had grown out of the
great hall, displayed a new lightness of touch. Windows, instead
of being mere slits or round-headed shuttered openings, were now
lancet-shaped, with pointed heads, and sometimes, in the private
rooms that were above the level of the great hall, there would be
panes of horn, ground thin, and set with lead in iron bars.

To reach these private rooms, a stairway of wood might rise to a
gallery, running across one end of the great hall. A window in the
lord's retiring room would give a view of the great hall. People
still seemed indifferent to noise, and did not mind hearing the
sounds of life—talking, singing, and the barking of dogs—that
came from the great hall every night when the household gathered
around the fire. The idea of completely separate rooms, cut off
from the core of the house, developed slowly. The lord's household was a great family; the lord was its head; and he wanted to keep
in touch with it and to see how it fared.

INTERIOR OF NORMAN HALL

The communal life of the great hall was not attended by many comforts.
Unglazed windows, high up in the wall, admitted light, rain, snow and wind:
a great fire built on a hearth in the centre begrimed everything with smoke:
the stone floor was covered with rushes, and above it on a raised platform the
high table was set, where the lord of the castle sat in state with his relatives
and guests.

It was natural for the first type of country house to be irregular in shape. Its buildings wandered about, and, half-house, half-castle, it was always being rebuilt and enlarged. In some parts of the country farm buildings were large and well constructed. The farmer's comfort and welfare depended on his landlord. The households of some fortunate farmers are described in the early twelfth century leases of the manors of St. Paul's. "The lessees were mostly the canons themselves or their relatives, and the stock and the buildings were evidently of exceptional excellence."[1] The quarters of a farmer's household were at least equal to those of a first-class manor. There was a hall, a "camera" (for sleep and retirement), and next to this the "domus" (or private dwelling). The separate buildings, all of one story, were grouped about one or more yards, and linked up by passages or pent-houses. A granary, kitchen, hay-house and stable were near the hall. The furniture received by the household included "4 casks, 3 cups, a boiler, a bench, a stool, 2 tables; also some well-seasoned wood."[2]

Kitchens were well supplied with utensils. There were cauldrons and pots, tripods for suspending them above the fire, frying pans, saucepans, and gridirons. A well equipped kitchen would have dishes of various sizes, a hand-mill, a pepper-mill, a bread-grater, a mortar and pestle, and a table for mincing and chopping herbs and vegetables.[3]

Although the peasants were still abominably housed—their cottages accommodated animals, as well as men, women and children—farm buildings were greatly improved when more peaceful conditions were established in the countryside. The castle was not the only large, secure country house: the fortified manor appeared, and in addition to a watch tower, it had its great central hall or house-place, round which private rooms were grouped. It had fireplaces, and, very rarely, a few glazed windows. Stone was still the chief material used for building, but it seems likely that the art of making bricks had been re-established in England at an early date. For example, in 1210, at Coggeshall Abbey in Essex, bricks were used and, although they may have been imported from Flanders, it is quite possible that English brick-making may have been started again. "The connection of Eastern England with Flanders was close and continuous. Still, was it not more likely that for brick-making, as well as for weaving and other crafts, not only the material itself, but also the makers thereof, had been imported?"[4]

Among the most powerful influences in the growth of domestic building were the inventions and experiments that were being made

[1] *Mediaeval England*, by Mary Bateson, Chap. V, p. 119. [2] *Ibid.*, p. 120.
[3] Thomas Wright, in his *History of Domestic Manners*, quotes an account of kitchen furniture, made by Alexander Neckam.
[4] *Tattershall Castle, Lincolnshire*, A Historical and Descriptive Survey by the late Lord Curzon and H. Avary Tipping, Chap. III, p. 48.

in the building of great churches. All the talent and inventiveness of craftsmen were encouraged by the Church and everything that went to the enriching of the inside and outside of churches was reflected in due time in the decoration, and in the very shape and form, of country houses, and in the streets of every city. For example, windows gradually increased in size, as builders made more experiments in enlarging the windows in churches. Church building was carried to the point when the church itself became a huge lantern of thin stone ribs, framing masses of coloured glass. Although this elaborate development of window spaces was spread over more than three centuries, it proceeded much faster in the twelfth and thirteenth centuries in church building than it did in domestic building. In the fortified manor, windows still had to be mean and narrow. In the towns, where houses were sheltered by the town walls, windows could expand, and they were of horn, framed in thin, flat, channelled strips of lead. It was the lead-worker's job to glaze windows. To this day, plumbers are also glaziers, and this association arose from the handling of the lead-framed, diamond-shaped panes of horn or glass that filled the windows of mediaeval houses.

The peasants' cottages were unaffected by all these inventions and improvements. Such dwellings have been described as "decrepit hovels, with rotten beams and half-ruined walls."[1] Thieves could break in through the walls of these miserable structures, and there is a record of a man being killed at his own fireside by some marauder thrusting a spear through the side of the house.[2] Chimneys were almost unknown, and the smoke oozed out of crevices in the wall or the roof. "The fire was made, either on the bare floor, or on an iron plate placed on the floor, and the peasants cooked and lived as best they could in a 'ful sooty' atmosphere."[3] The floor was of stamped and rammed earth, strewn with straw. There were a few stools, a trestle table, possibly a chest. Often the peasant's possessions, such as they were, would be stowed away in baskets.[4] Living in these insecure homes, with few possessions and no comforts the lot of the peasant in Norman England would appal the modern farm labourer or factory worker; it was a poor life, unless the feudal lord was really a responsible father to the vast family of people who depended upon him, and took a kindly interest in their welfare. Ferocious bullies, like Scott's Front-de-Boeuf in *Ivanhoe* were probably more common than Kipling's Sir Richard Dalyngridge and Gilbert de Aquila in *Puck of Pook's Hill*.

In the towns, the poorer classes had better accommodation, although the conditions of living were less healthy. In London,

[1] *The Mediaeval Village*, by G. G. Coulton, Chap. IX, p. 100. This description is quoted by Dr. Coulton from *Magna Vita S. Hugonis*.
[2] *Life on the English Manor*, by H. S. Bennett, Chap. IX, p. 230.
[3] *Ibid.*, Chap. IX, p. 228.　　　　　　　　　　[4] *Ibid.*, pp. 232–233.

gardens and trees and palaces adorned the city; the Thames was a sparkling highway, and the houses had spread beyond the cramping ring of the walls. Writing of London late in the twelfth century, William Fitzstephen, the close friend and biographer of Thomas á Becket, gave a pleasant picture of the city. He described a continuous suburb, lying between the city wall and the king's palace at Westminster. "On all sides, without the houses of the suburbs, are the citizens' gardens and orchards, planted with trees, both large, sightly, and adjoining together. On the north side are pastures and plain meadows, with brooks running through them, turning watermills with a pleasant noise. Not far off is a great forest, a well wooded chase, having good covert for harts, bucks, does, boars and wild bulls. The corn fields are not of a hungry sandy mould, but as the fruitful fields of Asia, yielding plentiful increase, and filling the barns with corn. There are near London, on the north side, especial wells in the surburbs, sweet, wholesome, and clear. Amongst which, Holywell, Clarkenwell, and St. Clement's well, are most famous, and most frequented by scholars and youths of the city in summer evenings, when they walk forth to take the air."[1]

But Fitzstephen ignored a good many defects, possibly because he was used to them. For example: "In the mediaeval town only the wider streets were paved. A 'kennel' or open drain ran down the middle of most streets and the ground was continually sodden with filth and refuse of all kinds. The shallow wells and the streams and rivers, which were usually the source of water supplies, were constantly polluted. In London, by the thirteenth century, the supply of drinking water was so obviously inadequate that Henry III gave the citizens permission 'to convey water from the town of Tybourne by pipes of lead into the city'. Two conduits were then built and later others were added by private enterprise but as they were open channels for the greater part of their courses, they were constantly polluted."[2]

London had its third great fire in 1077 and its fourth ten years later. Another great fire occurred in 1132 and another in 1136. In 1212, the seventh great fire of London did an enormous amount of damage and attempts were made to check this constantly recurring danger. The steps taken were so successful that only three great fires have since occurred—in 1264, 1666 and 1940. Stone buildings now appeared more frequently in London and other cities. William the Conqueror had built the Tower, and churches and palaces were now largely in stone. The houses that lined the streets were still mainly of timber and plaster but stone party walls were

[1] William Fitzstephen's biography of Becket, *Vita Sancti Thomae*, includes an account of London in the preface which is entitled "Descriptio Nobilisimae civitatis Londoniae". John Stow, in his *Survey of London* (1603), includes the passage quoted above in the section, "The Suburbs without the Walls".

[2] *Sanitation Through the Ages*, by Desmond Eyles, *The Official Architect*, Vol. 4, No. 4, April 1941, p. 165.

soon the rule, and various building regulations were made. In 1189, Fitz Ailwyne, the first Mayor of London, gave the city its first Building Act, which was known as Fitz-Ailwyne's Assize. Under this, thatch was prohibited and stone party walls were made compulsory. For some centuries this law was either ignored or evaded.

There was a tendency in town houses for the framework to project as the storeys ascended, so that in a narrow street, above the first floor level, the houses would lean towards each other. Between the timber framework there would be plaster and, at a later date, and in the Eastern Counties, bricks. Town houses would be built by skilled craftsmen; each belonging to his protective guild, joiners, masons, plasterers, men who took an immense pride in their work and who were compelled, by the high standards set by their guilds, to execute good work.

Glass was rare, but horn ground into thin sheets, was used in windows. Although the open fire still distributed its smoke throughout rooms, the hearth on which it was built was sometimes set against the wall and a hole made immediately above. The upper rooms, when the house was of two or three storeys, were protected from smoke by their walls being boxed forward so that smoke trickled up and found its way out through the hole in the roof, more or less guided in its path. It was a rudimentary flue, and from it the chimney breast developed.

The furniture of the large town house was improving. The shut bedstead and the independent bedstead were made more comfortable with feather mattresses, though many people still slept on straw. There were benches and stools, trestle tables and chests with hinged lids, bound with iron and fitted with locks. The locksmith was becoming an important craftsman. Tallow candles were fairly common but wax candles were used almost exclusively in churches. The former consisted of flax fibre or rushes dipped in melted and strained tallow. (Two of the London livery companies were concerned with candle-making: the Waxchandlers and the Tallowchandlers.) Woven and embroidered fabrics enriched and warmed the walls of rooms. The house of the rich merchant, although it might be his place of business, and be over his shop or warehouse, contained as many luxuries and comforts as the nobleman's palace or castle.

In the towns there was a great deal of communal feeding in taverns. Among the town-dwellers, the artisans and tradesmen, and their dependents and apprentices, a new civic sense was growing. In a few generations it was expressed by the pride they took in building, not only fine houses, but great guild halls and market-places.

NORMAN CASTLE WITH MOAT AND KEEP.

CHAPTER V

MEDIAEVAL ENGLISH HOMES
(A.D. 1250-1450)

FROM 1250 to 1450 the country grew richer, the cities larger and wealthier, the countryside more secure, and the homes of nobleman, farmer, merchant and artisan more convenient and comfortable. Civilisation, except in the border country in the North, was settling into a period of order and growth. But in Northumberland, Durham, Cumberland, Westmorland, and northern Yorkshire, even the small country house was still a stronghold, with its watch tower, and thick outer walls and narrow windows, high above ground level. The gloom of fortification also darkened houses and castles on the borders of Wales. But elsewhere, the castle became a more cheerful place, and the fortified manor house and the larger farmhouse were real homes.

During those two centuries, when craftsmen were making sturdy buildings, and ornamenting them with skill and imagination, the rise of English civilisation was violently and terribly interrupted by the Black Death, the Bubonic Plague that destroyed half the population in 1348-1349, and left the country with empty villages and untended fields. Everyone suffered, for nobleman and peasant alike lived in conditions that favoured the spread of disease. Labour was scarce, and despite attempts to fix wages, the peasant was at last able to demand and receive a slightly better reward for his work.

Some parts of the country never recovered from the Plague. Norfolk and Suffolk, for example, have been thinly populated ever since, and in those counties it is not unusual to see some tiny village served by a vast church, which was built when a thriving community used it, and a small town flourished where now only a few cottages line a short street. But although so many people died in the middle of the fourteenth century, the building of churches, and the enlarging of the great cathedrals continued.

The Early English period of Gothic architecture ended in the mid-thirteenth century; the Decorated period began in the fourteenth, and the Perpendicular period in the fifteenth century. Although the churches took the best that craftsmen could give, and the work of masons and carpenters was partly an act of worship when they were building some new part of a great church, there was plenty of skill left over for the making of fine houses.

The fourteenth century manor house would still have a moat,

though the bridge over it would often be permanent.[1] Passing over this bridge and through the gate-house, which would retain its portcullis and its thick gates, the visitor would enter a central courtyard, around which buildings were grouped. These buildings shouldered against each other; they had a friendly, rather haphazard air, as though they had been put up as need for them arose, as indeed they had, for the manor house was always growing. Opposite the gate-house, the great hall occupied one side of the courtyard, and it would be entered through a porch. Tall windows admitted light to the hall, and although glass was seldom used except in churches, the windows were divided into small sections by stone uprights, called mullions, and cross-pieces, called transomes. These small sections could easily be protected against the weather by wooden shutters. Horn panes, fixed in lead frames, sometimes filled in the space between the mullions. The head of the window was a pointed arch, and the mullions running up to it branched into a criss-cross of curves, which formed geometric patterns, so that a number of small, ornamental lights sparkled at the window top, in a variety of shapes, crosses, rosettes and circles. This form of stonework decoration in windows is known as tracery.

The inside of the hall was now well lit and no longer darkened by smoke, for the central hearth had become old-fashioned. The fireplace now occupied a big section of the wall, and above it a large hood projected from the wall and guided the smoke, and much of the heat, up the chimney. That fire, fed with charcoal, wood and turf, was seldom allowed to go out; it remained, glowing on a pile of ashes, night and day, sometimes for years. The stonework of the fire-place and hearth was always warm. Thick walls helped to keep up the temperature in the great hall, and the chill was taken off the stonework by embroidered wall hangings.

The hall was often lofty, and the roof was carried on great ribs of timber, for the "crucks" which had replaced the posts in the earliest forms of roof construction, had grown into huge arches, and the carpenter had become a bold engineer, bridging wide spaces with the material over which he had gained such mastery.

The porch was separated from the great hall by a wooden screen which supported a gallery and protected the hall from the cold air of the porch; behind it were doors leading to the kitchen, the buttery, pantry and larder. The screen was pierced by two or three doors, so hot food could be brought quickly from the kitchen to the hall. The gallery over the screen accommodated minstrels who entertained the company.

The great hall was still the core of the country dwelling, whether it was a castle or a fortified manor house. Many people still lived and

[1] *Social Life in the Days of Piers Plowman*, by D. Chadwick, Chap. III, "Country Life", p. 53.

slept in it; and although there were other rooms to which the master and mistress of the house could retire, guests were entertained in the great hall on that exclusive part, the däis, which raised a few privileged people above the straw and rushes.

The hall occupied the whole height of the building. Stairways of stone, in the thickness of the wall, or winding up inside turrets built specially to take stairs, led to the private rooms: the lady's bower, and some spare rooms, in which beds could be made up for guests. The solar, or withdrawing room, still retained a connection with the hall, though this was no longer a window, and had been reduced to a small peep-hole.

Towards the end of the fourteenth century, the sociable habits of the country household were changing. William Langland, the English poet who was born in 1332, wrote about the changes that had come to the land. He lived in a period of discontent and revolution, which flared up in 1381 when Wat Tyler and his followers rebelled in an attempt to abolish serfdom. "Private chamber and chimney corner were beginning to attract the lord and lady from the hall."[1] In the poet's own words:

"There the lorde ne the lady liketh noute to sytte."

The "pryve parloure" or the "chambre with a chymneye" was now the setting of a more exclusive form of life. This solar, which had originally been a kind of bed-sitting room, ceased to be merely a private refuge from the life of the hall. It provided the background for the lord and the lady; the simple pleasures of eating and drinking were no longer shared by the household, nor did the lord's dependents share in the new standards of comfort established in those private and forbidden rooms.

The country house was not always owned by a nobleman or his relatives. The merchants of London grew increasingly prosperous in the well-ordered England of the fourteenth and early fifteenth centuries. One of the most famous houses that have survived, Penshurst Place in Kent, was built by a London merchant in 1341. Like all English houses, it grew century by century. To-day the great hall is much as it was in the reign of Edward III, but the woodwork screens are Elizabethan. Although fire-places had been in use for over a century, the great hall of Penshurst Place had the old-time central hearth, with a lantern-shaped louvre in the roof to let out smoke.

Furniture was still simple in form, and there was little variety about it. There were chests, which were also used as seats, and benches, stools, trestle tables, boxes and baskets. Chairs with high, straight backs were used, but they were very rare. Washing was done chiefly in basins. There was not much privacy about bathing, and a bath

[1] *Social Life in the Days of Piers Plowman*, by D. Chadwick, p. 55.

43

in a large wooden tub, was often taken in company. The oldest English book on hunting, *The Master of Game*, written between 1406 and 1413, by Edward III's grandson, Edward, second Duke of York, describes the thoroughness of the hunter's toilet after the exertions of the chase. When the hunter has come home, "he shall doff his clothes and his shoes and his hose, and he shall wash his thighs and his legs, and peradventure all his body. And in the meanwhile he shall order well his supper, with *wortes* (roots) *and of the neck* of the hart and of other good meats, and good wine *or ale*. And when he hath well eaten and drunk he shall be glad and well, and well at his ease. And then shall he take the air in the evening of the night, for the great heat that he hath had. And then he shall go and drink and lie in his bed in fair fresh clothes, and shall sleep well and steadfastly all the night . . ."[1]

To sleep "well and steadfastly" was easy enough on a feather bed, but bags of straw or flock were usually the hard surfaces on which people slept. Sheets were in general use, and coverlets of a rough material called dagswain were common. Pillows were stuffed with feathers, but very often a shaped piece of wood was used as a pillow. Anything approaching the soft and yielding surfaces of modern chairs and settees was unknown. Sometimes thick fabrics would be doubled up to act as cushions on the top of a chest, but upholstery had not been invented.

Candles, rush-lights and flaring torches were still the chief methods of lighting rooms at night; but this lack of good artificial light was not a hardship in an age when few people could read or write, and a large fire-place with abundant wood fuel provided not only heat but a cheerful glare. In the kitchen of the country house, a huge open fire-place would devour fuel. The preparation of meals had become an art, and the kitchen was a well-equipped and important workshop. A large trestle table would be the chief piece of furniture, and there would be racks and hooks for pots, pans, cauldrons, ladles, basins, jugs and baskets. A revolving spit would be turned by hand or dog-power, a dog being shut up in a cylindrical cage, forming a treadmill which moved the spit as the dog paddled the cage round and round. Suspended from the ceiling beams were sides of bacon and salted beef, hams, dried fish, and bunches of herbs.

In the farmhouse, the kitchen was the hall or house place. The farmer was the modest counterpart of the lord of the manor, and was master of his household. The life of the farm kitchen was as communal as life in the great hall of the manor or castle had once been, and although sleeping chambers for the farmer and his wife

---

[1] *The Master of Game*, by Edward, Second Duke of York, edited by W. A. and F. Baillie-Grohman, with a foreword by Theodore Roosevelt. (London, 1909), Chap. I, p. II.

OUTDOOR COOKING

Mediaeval peasants did much of their cooking out-of-doors, with such devices
as the primitive turning spit shown here.

adjoined the kitchen, the farmer was not separated from the lives and
troubles of the people who worked on the farm lands. He knew all
about them, and was a hard-working and responsible master. The
kitchen fire-place was the cheerful rallying-point for social life at the
farm. All our ideas of comfort and cheerful company are linked up
with the open fire: love of the fireside is a very old English habit,
and it has left its mark upon the shape and character of English
houses, large and small.

The farmer became the real lord of the land, for after the Black
Death, labour was so scarce that the big land-owners took to
sheep-farming. They had been scared by Wat Tyler's rebellion,
although they had managed to suppress it by force. Sheep-farming
called for far less labour; the land-owner no longer wanted to be
troubled with the business of growing crops and managing labour;
so the villein who had hitherto given service to the land-owner,
was allowed to rent land, for cash payments, and become a farmer
himself. These new farmers, who were called yeomen, did not own
the land they farmed, but as tenants paying rent to the landlord,
they enjoyed a new and welcome freedom. The landowners, relieved
of the task of running the day-to-day work of their estates, and
drawing their farm-rents and profits from sheep farming, had far
more leisure and wealth than they had ever enjoyed before. Much
of their wealth they spent on building; by the beginning of the
fifteenth century, the country house had become a collection of
rooms, well-appointed, comfortable, and no longer clustering around
a great hall. The house place still existed; the hall was still a large
chamber; but its social life had altered. It was used for feasting and
entertainment; but the idea of the great household, with the lord
as benevolent father of it, was out of date. The nobility and gentry
acquired an ever-increasing array of possessions; their life became

more elaborate and elegant; and the yeoman farmer took over their ancient partnership with the men who lived and worked on the land. Even the peasant, whose lot had been improved as a result of the labour shortage which followed the pestilence, began to collect a few more possessions. But although standards of living were raised a little for some peasants, the latter part of the fourteenth century was an unhappy time for the poor. In *Piers Plowman*, Langland draws a depressing picture of their lot. In the poor man's "cote straw and a blanket did service for a bed, but sometimes there was only straw. No cupboards or coffers accommodated his possessions . . . all the family treasures were contained in baskets."[1]

Langland describes an England in which extreme poverty and extravagant wealth appeared side by side. The towns were prosperous, and the nobility, recklessly pursuing luxury, were putting money into the pockets of the merchants, so that the merchant class gradually secured some of the privileges which had formerly been enjoyed only by noblemen. Clothes became increasingly elaborate, and enormous sums were spent on food and the preparation of prolonged and elaborate feasts. Langland suggests that even the labourers, especially at harvest time, lived extravagantly on good, wholesome food. "Amongst the luxuries of the age, the poet mentions cups and goblets of silver and pure gold. High houses were regarded as a good investment for money."[2]

In the towns, high houses were certainly bringing in money to landlords. Storey was piled on storey, though the streets still remained narrow, and were often dark and shaded lanes, overshadowed by these increasingly tall, timber-framed, plaster-faced buildings, that brought such a rich harvest of rents to the pockets of the merchants who owned them.

Not only did big mercantile centres like London flourish and grow, but townships arose round monasteries and universities. The London merchant was becoming a man of taste. When he built a country house, like Penshurst Place, only the best was good enough for him; and the arts of building in the late fourteenth century advanced rapidly. His town house was spacious; for although London had crowded and narrow streets, the country came into the city; fields and gardens, orchards and grooves of trees mingled with the clusters of houses, so the city was, even within its walls, a patchwork of grey stone, coloured plaster and green leaves.

The plastering of walls, inside and out, had originally been a precaution against fire. The fear of fire haunted the towns and cities of the Middle Ages. The use of thatch for new buildings in London had been forbidden as early as 1212, and at that time the city council had made an order that all cookshops on the Thames were to be

[1] *Social Life in the Days of Piers Plowman*, by D. Chadwick, Section V, p. 82.
[2] *Ibid.*, p. 81.

plastered. A cookshop was often the starting place of a fire. Plastering became a recognised craft, and it was used to provide a good surface for painting. Houses were often whitewashed outside, and the inside walls were painted, sometimes with great skill, so the rooms of a large town house would be enriched with colour. The London merchants were actively engaged in foreign trade, and a variety of luxurious materials were imported from overseas; fabrics, metal-work and glass came into the warehouses of London, together with spices and furs. Wood-work, elaborately carved by English and Flemish craftsmen, appeared in sitting-rooms and bedrooms; chests and coffers were ornamental as well as useful; and on such pieces of furniture, the tracery that had been worked out by masons in stone for the tall windows of churches was reproduced in miniature, so the front of a chest would suggest a row of blind, pointed windows. Roundels of chip carving, in geometric patterns would also be used to ornament chests; but there was plenty of bold figure carving, and spirited scenes were sometimes portrayed. Linen and clothes were stored in chests, and a small shelf on one side, near the top of a chest, would be fixed to take little bags of dried herbs or leaves that would scent the contents. (The practice of drying woodruff, which smells like new-mown hay, and sewing it up in bags which are put into linen cupboards, still survives in some parts of the country.)

The joiner and carpenter were the two most important craftsmen in the building of town houses; the tiler or bricklayer and the plasterer completed their work, for most houses consisted of a stout wooden skeleton that supported floors and roof, filled in with rubble (odds and ends of loose stonework) and plastered over. Small neat bricks, set in mortar, sometimes occupied the space between the timber uprights, though bricks were rarely used outside the Eastern Counties. Roofs were tiled, with stone or clay tiles. The timber framing of the house was not concealed; it was frequently orna-mented with carved patterns. These timber-framed houses looked comfortable; and even when they were three or four storeys high, they were safe, for the timber framework locked the floors and walls together, and gave the whole building stability. Only when they were built badly, the framework skimped, and the plastering slapped on carelessly, did they have a short life. "It frequently happened that all the wood-and-plaster houses in a street fell into decay. Such a street was then called Rotten Row, or 'ruinous street'."[1] High houses, as Langland had said, were a good investment; floor piled on floor brought in more rent, and the landlord who went in for speculative building often ran up houses as cheaply as possible. The slum is not a modern invention; it is almost as old as greed.

Most of the streets in the more densely populated parts of the

[1] *The Evolution of the English House*, by S. O. Addy, Chap. VI, p. 120 (1933, enlarged edition).

A MEDIAEVAL STREET SCENE

Houses built of timber and daubed with painted plaster leaned towards each other: stalls often thronged and obstructed the narrow streets of the town, giving them the likeness of an oriental bazaar. Narrow, overcrowded, irregular in form, the houses in these streets blazed with colour.

mediaeval city would seem like slums to modern eyes. The houses were all individual; there were no terraces, nothing linked a house with its neighbour. Some leant forward over the muddy, filthy roadway; others stood back behind walls, that enclosed a courtyard. The street was partly blocked with stairways, that led down to cellars or to taverns. The shopkeepers and stall-holders regarded the street as a customer trap, and did their best to prevent through-traffic, for they wanted to collect a crowd round their own particular display of merchandise. It has been suggested that these trading streets were like bazaars, and with their congestion, their colour and movement, their noise and smell, they certainly had the diversity of an oriental bazaar.[1] The small shopkeepers and their apprentices, the artisans and craftsmen who lived in the upper storeys of those tall houses, looked daily upon such scenes. They were better off than the peasants in the matter of food, shelter and possessions; they could eat at the cookshops, those taverns that lay in cellars below the street level; they lived in better houses, and they had a greater variety of furniture—stools, benches, trestle tables, chests and possibly store cupboards. Tallow candles gave them light when the windows were shuttered; if they had a room in a well-built house, they could have a fire in cold weather, and sit round the hooded fire-place.

All over the country towns were growing. Some were acquiring wealth from the expanding wool trade. Villages like Chipping Campden in Gloucestershire were adorned with handsome houses in stone; Lavenham in Suffolk reflected the prosperity of its cloth trade in the beauty and scale of its buildings. Such places were cities in miniature, small, compact, set like jewels in the Cotswold valleys and rich East Anglian levels.

Small town houses were built everywhere by the new class of merchants and traders, the business men who were not big enough to have the power or standing of the great London merchants, but who formed a separate community, and whose wealth gave them social independence. These men wanted power; but power was still in the hands of the nobility and the landowning gentry. These traders created new wealth, and by catering for the extravagant tastes of their social superiors, they also acquired wealth from the nobility. They used some of it to build themselves homes in the towns and cities where they worked, and their houses were also their places of business. Employing local materials and local labour, they gave craftsmen a fresh outlet for their skill, and throughout England a new type of home came into existence. It lacked the spaciousness of the manor house, and the communal cheerfulness of the farmhouse; it was not a survival from an earlier period, nor was it designed to imitate the splendours of a nobleman's palace

[1] *The Evolution of the English House*, by S. O. Addy, Chap. VI, p. 112.

or great country house: it was a modest, but entirely comfortable home, and all the knowledge woodworkers and masons and smiths had accumulated in the building of churches was available to make that home not only comfortable but beautiful.

Those mediaeval Englishmen seemed incapable of doing ugly or stupid things when they built; their houses were splendidly fit for their purpose, and materials were used to the best advantage and with a quick-witted skill. Although the forests had been slowly shrinking, century by century, as trees were cut down, and no systematic replanting took place, England was still a country with an abundant supply of timber, and it was the chief building material. In domestic architecture it was the age of oak and plaster: it was soon, except in those parts of the country where local stone supplied the builders' need, to become the age of brick.

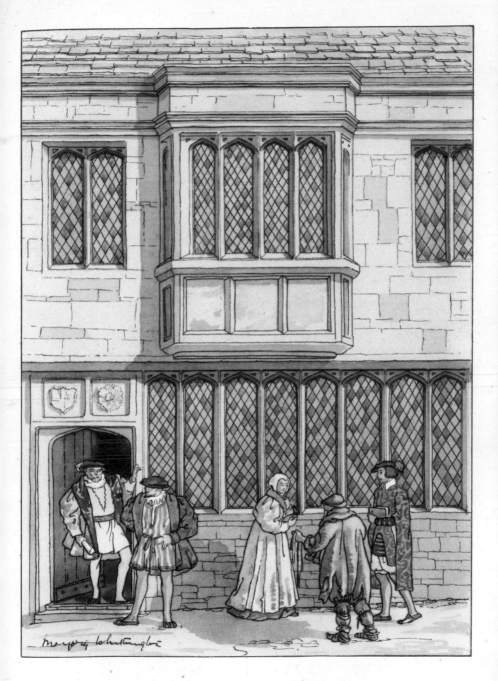

EARLY TUDOR TOWN HOUSE.

CHAPTER VI

EARLY TUDOR HOUSES
(A.D. 1450–1558)

IN the last half of the fifteenth century and the first half of the sixteenth, immense changes took place in the social, religious and economic life of England. From Jack Cade's rebellion in 1450 to the death of Mary Tudor in 1558, power and wealth came into new hands, for the old nobility practically committed suicide as a class in the Wars of the Roses, and after the dissolution of the monasteries by Henry VIII hundreds of new landowning families were established in the country. During that time Gothic architecture came to an end; ideas were imported from abroad, and foreign craftsmen, Flemish, French and Italian, came to England to practise them. The members of the new aristocracy who set the fashions in clothes, in house building and furnishing, became "Italianate" in their taste, for in Italy the architecture and learning of ancient Rome were being splendidly revived by gifted artists and scholars, and this Italian Renaissance was influencing all Europe. Not only did ideas change about the design of town and country houses; abroad the nature of the town itself was changed, for streets were widened and improved in many European cities, and in England, Sir Thomas More, (who was the H. G. Wells of his day) described an ideal city in the second book of his *Utopia* (1516).

Writing of this imaginary city of Amaurote, he said: "The streets be appointed and set forth very commodious and handsome, both for carriage, and also against the winds. The houses be of fair and gorgeous building, and on the street side they stand joined together in a long row through the whole street without any partition or separation. The streets be twenty feet broad. On the back side of the houses through the whole length of the street, lie large gardens inclosed round about with the back part of the streets. Every house hath two doors, one into the street, and a postern door on the back side into the garden. These doors be made with two leaves, never locked nor bolted, so easy to be opened, that they will follow the least drawing of a finger, and shut again alone."

Sir Thomas More's description of the houses in his Utopian city reflected not only the taste of his own time, which favoured an increasing richness in building, but displayed a practical regard for fire-proof and weather-proof materials. Those houses were "curiously builded after a gorgeous and gallant sort, with three storeys one over another. The outsides of the walls be made either of hard

EARLY TUDOR INTERIOR

Once the need for fortification passed, windows were enormously enlarged.
The small, lead-bound panes were enriched with roundels of coloured glass,
generally bearing heraldic devices.

flint, or of plaster, or else of brick, and the inner sides be well strengthened with timber work. The roofs be plain and flat, covered with a certain kind of plaster that is of no cost, and yet so tempered that no fire can hurt or perish it, and withstandeth the violence of the weather better than any lead. They keep the wind out of their windows with glass, for it is there much used, and some-times also with fine linen cloth dipped in oil or amber, and that for two commodities. For by this means more light cometh in, and the wind is better kept out."

Houses of "a gorgeous and gallant sort" arose all over England after the Wars of the Roses had exhausted the nobility, and the armies that had marched and counter-marched across the land were demobilised. A strong government under a new type of king prom-ised greater security to the country as a whole; and because power was stripped from individual noblemen, private armies and private warfare were no longer possible.

All need for fortification had vanished. Thick walls, heavy gates, mean but safe windows, stagnant and often insanitary moats, were, in a generation, to become relics of the past. The moats were filled in, gardens took their place, windows expanded, and a new, light, pleasant and characteristically English architecture enriched the countryside with houses of brick and stone. Although they still followed the rather rambling outlines of the castle and were closely akin to the fortified manor house, they proved that architecture had shaken off fear. These new houses also showed the special English genius for creating homes. Large manor houses, like Ockwells in Berkshire, and Compton Wynyates in Warwickshire, the original Tudor parts of Hampton Court Palace, St. James's Palace, all that remains of the old royal palace on Richmond Green, the Bishop's Palace at Ely, Sutton Place at Guildford, and smaller buildings like Denver Hall on the road from Ely to Lynn in Norfolk, all possess an inviting, cosy and settled air. No previous period of English build-ing had brought this friendly appearance to such perfection.

After 1450 Gothic architecture had entered what is known as the Perpendicular period. Churches and cathedrals were tall and slender: they had become thin frameworks for holding glass, and they have been described as cages of stone.[1] The big half-timbered country house was a cage of oak, a robust wooden framework for bricks and glass. The builders of country houses seemed eager to bring as much daylight as possible into rooms. Tall bay windows rose from the ground to the roof line; on the lower floors windows often extended along the upper part of the outside wall, so that light would pour through the frieze above the panelling in a room, as well as through the small, diamond-shaped panes between the stone or oak mullions of the bay window.

[1] The phrase was used by W. R. Lethaby.

COTTAGES AT DEREHAM, NORFOLK

These thatched, two-storied cottages were built in the early sixteenth century, though the band of decorative plaster-work and the windows with the rectangular glass panes have been added at a later date.

Many country houses were built of warm red brickwork. Bricks were set in courses, and a system was worked out to bind or bond the wall into a firm mass. This bonding consisted of laying the bricks in every course to cover the joints in the course below. There are different kinds of bond, the commonest being English bond and Flemish bond. The long part of a brick is called a stretcher, and the end part a header. In English bond, alternate courses of headers and stretchers are used: in Flemish, there are headers and stretchers in each course. Some bricks were burnt extra hard so that they became blue-black in colour, and these were called vitreous bricks. Patterns were sometimes made in walls, by inserting vitreous headers in different courses, so diamond-shaped devices, crosses and chequering, decorated the brickwork. (Good examples of this form of decoration may be seen in the Tudor parts of Hampton Court Palace.) Sometimes stretchers were laid to form herring-bone patterns, often in the brick interiors of fire-places.

Though many big country houses were built throughout of stone, in the brickmaking areas stone would be used only for the framing

A TUDOR FARM

Farmhouses during the sixteenth century grew larger and more convenient: they were often built of permanent materials. The upper storey in this example is half-timbered, but the ground floor and the outbuildings are of stone. (See page 57.)

of doors and windows. Various building inventions were made, and one of the most important was the bay window, which was really a three-sided glazed extension of a room, which not only gave light to the interior, but provided a sunny, sheltered sitting place. The oriel window was a bay which projected from the first or second storey of a house, and was built out from the wall, overhanging the ground below.

Conveniences and luxuries hitherto confined to the town house, now found their way into the country. In those houses of brick and stone, the rooms would be panelled with wood, and men and women lived against a background of golden coloured oak. This panelling was a plain, regular framework that clothed the wall agreeably, but sometimes the panels were carved with ornament. On chests, where linen was stored, the front panels were often carved with a device to represent folded linen. This "linen-fold" pattern was greatly varied, and in time it was used on wall panelling and cupboard fronts. A favourite form of ornament was the vine, and leaves and tendrils and bunches of grapes were carved on beams, both inside and outside houses. Above the panelling and below the ceiling, a plaster frieze might have hunting scenes modelled on it, and decorative patterns in which flowers, leaves, fruit and animals were intermingled. These would be gaily coloured, and occasionally heraldic devices would appear on the frieze. In the windows, the regular diamond-patterned panes would sometimes be broken by roundels of stained glass, also bearing some heraldic device.

The fire-place was of stone, in the form of a wide, pointed archway, with a little carving on it; the interior would be lined with brick or stone, and the fire built directly upon a raised hearth, the logs supported between a pair of iron dogs. The efficiency of the fire was increased by a flue which was enclosed in a chimney stack, and this brickwork stack rose above the roof level and bore aloft tall chimneys of cut and moulded brickwork. Three or four flues from the fire-places of different rooms, would be carried up in one stack, and a cluster of chimneys would add to the decorative effect of the roof. William Harrison, Rector of Radwinter and Canon of Windsor, in his *Description of England*, first published in 1577 and re-issued and amended ten years later, could still write of chimneys as novel features in house building. "There are old men yet dwelling in the village where I remaine," he said, "which have noted three things to be marvellously altered in England within their sound remembrance . . . One is, the multitude of chimnies latelie erected, whereas in their young daies there was not above two or three, if so many, in most . . . towns of the realme (the religious houses and manuor places of their lords alwaies excepted, and peradventure some great personages) but each one made his fire against a reredosse in the hall where he dined and dressed his meat."[1]

For a generation or so, before rich Englishmen became "Italianate" a native style of building was developing, both in brick and stone. At the beginning of the Tudor period the fancy of building craftsmen was unhampered by any foreign fashion; they carved wood and stone, moulded plaster and painted patterns on it, with all the freedom they had exercised in their adornment of mediaeval churches; for although the work of mediaeval English craftsmen was rigidly controlled by the laws and regulations of their guilds, they were given a fairly free hand with ornament. The pleasure of ornamenting came after the exacting work of building was done, and the materials had been used according to the standards laid down by the guilds; carving and painting were recreations; and a vigorous sense of humour was sometimes displayed, even in the treatment of church woodwork. There was a fine sense of order in the decoration of houses in this very early Tudor period, and it was destroyed when craftsmen were given foreign patterns to copy. The English Gothic tradition lasted until Elizabethan days, and in some parts of the west country and East Anglia, it survived well into the seventeenth century, and even later.

The interior of the house had now lost its old simplicity, and

[1] The spelling of some words in this and subsequent quotations from Harrison's *Description* has been modernised.

FARM OUTBUILDINGS

The stone outbuildings of the farm shown on page 55. This type of building changed very little from the late fifteenth to the early nineteenth century in localities where stone was plentiful.

there were many rooms, some large, some small, some leading out of each other. The hall was often the centre upon which all traffic converged, for the stairway was in it, and many rooms of the upper floors opened on to an encircling gallery to which the stairs ascended.

There was less difference now between the country house and the large town house; both shared new standards of furnishing and equipment. Some of the early Tudor furniture has survived, and it often reproduces in wood the type of ornament that had been worked out in stone in the last great buildings of the Gothic period. There were cupboards with panels of tracery, like small windows piercing the woodwork, food hutches and sideboard tables, which were really dwarf chests on short legs; also low standing cupboards. The chest was still the commonest article of furniture. There were trestle tables, and benches; but chairs were still unusual, although a new form of chair with an X-shaped frame had appeared. These X-shaped chairs had seats and backs of stretched fabric, and the entire framework may have been covered with fabric also. They were not upholstered, but the seat was yielding, and was rendered more comfortable by the addition of a loose cushion. Another type of chair, made entirely of oak, showed little advance on the throne-like

57

A FRIEZE WINDOW

High up in a room, above the panelling and below the ceiling, a long window often occupied the frieze in sixteenth-century country houses. Here is an example in a Tudor farmhouse.

mediaeval designs; it was a box, with arms and a straight back; sides, front and back would be panelled, and the linen-fold device might be used to decorate the panels.

In the bedroom, truckle beds were used; but the four-post bed, with a roof of its own, called a tester, a high wooden back running up to the tester, and curtains at the sides and ends, reproduced the characteristics of the shut-bed of earlier times. It was really a separate chamber when the heavy curtains were drawn, a room within a room, and it survived in all its stuffiness for nearly four centuries. Feather beds, quilts, sheets and pillows are common items in the inventories of the period; and a large number of people must have slept comfortably. The old men mentioned in Harrison's *Description of England* also marvelled at the increase of comfort in bedding. Harrison quotes them as saying: ". . . our fathers and we ourselves have lien full oft upon straw pallets, covered onlie with a sheet, under coverlets made of dagswain or hopharlots (I use their own termes) and a good round log under their heads instead of a bolster. If it were so that our fathers or the good man of the house, had a matteres or flockbed, and thereto a sacke of chaffe to rest his head upon, he thought himselfe to be as well lodged as the lord of the towne . . ."

The country house and the town house, lit by candles at night,

58

flooded with light from generous windows by day, had many comforts in common. In the rooms, oak panelled walls, carved ceiling beams, coloured plaster-work, rich fabrics, glazed windows, emblazoned with heraldic patches, and an abundance of well-made sturdy furniture in oak, created an impression of gaiety and utility. In those early Tudor homes, nothing was overdone; no article was over-burdened with decoration, and English craftsmen were using their native wood, oak, to the best advantage.

The country wood-worker also used other materials, for elm, yew and the fruit woods, apple and cherry, were available. Some time during the fifteenth century, the sycamore and the walnut had been introduced. As yet there was no shortage of timber, though the working of iron, especially in Sussex, made inroads on the forest that had once covered the Weald. But the needs of building and ironworking were not yet big enough to account for the steady shrinking of the forest lands: wood was still the chief form of fuel, which brought such cheap, abundant and cheerful comfort to the hearth of peasant, merchant, artisan and nobleman alike.

Comparatively few large houses were built in the towns, for the merchants preferred to move into the countryside and build there. Everywhere in the country, new building was going on; farmers added to their houses, landlords built better and larger cottages for their tenants, and the peasant for the first time began to live in a house with two storeys. In worldly goods the cottager was a little richer, and his cottage now often had a large and convenient fire-place, with a flue and a chimney, so cooking could be done without the interior of the house being made uninhabitable by smoke. A loft or a tiny bedroom below the thatch, approached by a ladder through a hole, was another luxury.

The cottage now had stools and a rough table, and one or more chests, also shelves for plates and vessels. It was still built mainly of timber and plaster, but occasionally of brick and timber. In Cornwall, the Mendips and the Cotswolds and in Yorkshire, a few stone cottages were built; though it was still a new and rather strange idea to use good building material for making permanent homes for people of low degree. The country was rich, and growing steadily richer. Land had been re-distributed after the dissolution of the monasteries, wealth had changed hands, and since the accession of Henry VII, much new wealth had been created by increasing trade. Nearly everybody except the dispossessed monks and the hordes of mendicants who had depended on the monasteries had some share in that new wealth.

The towns were growing, but they were not growing according to the spacious ideas suggested in Sir Thomas More's *Utopia*. They were still crowded and narrow, and the houses overhung the streets, the only large open spaces being those surrounding a church, or a

EARLY TUDOR FIREPLACE, CHAIR AND CHEST
The "linenfold" device is used on the wall panelling and on the arm-chair.

market hall. But there were still gardens and orchards here and there among the houses, and even in London the scent of the country, the smell of fields and trees, was never remote, for the city was not separated from the countryside by a vast belt of suburbs.

The small town house now had better windows, and they were often glazed, although glazing was still considered a great luxury; but in outward appearance and in the materials used for building, no change had taken place. Although the artisan, like the peasant, had more possessions and better furniture than his grandparents, his standards of life would make a twentieth-century factory operative shudder. Few houses had any sanitation; the water supply was irregular, and its sources were often tainted. The streets were foul and undrained.

But although the early sixteenth century English cities might offend the nose, they could never offend the eye. Tall, cramped houses, with pointed roofs and painted plaster fronts, lined the streets gaily, and from an aeroplane a city like London would have resembled some brightly coloured toy. Although it had become an age of brick and stone in the countryside, it was still the age of wood and plaster in the town.

CHAPTER VII

THE ELIZABETHAN HOME
(A.D. 1558–1603)

LIZABETH'S reign witnessed the most complicated and adventurous experiments in building. As usual, architecture was reflecting the changes that were taking place in social life; for England and its people were changing. The Italian Renaissance had brought back into the life of Europe the learning and the arts of the classic civilisation of Greece and Rome: in England the learning was adopted and the arts imitated, and the Elizabethan age became the Early Renaissance period of English architecture. But another and far stronger influence was changing the outlook and reshaping the ambitions of men. "The recovery of the classics opened a long and fair vista backwards; the exploration of the New World seemed to lift the curtain on a glorious future. And the English, the little parochial people, who for centuries had tilled their fields and tended their cattle in their island home, cut off from the great movements of European policy, suddenly found themselves, by virtue of their shipping, competitors for the domination of the earth. It is no wonder that their hearts distended with pride, and, hardening in their strength, gloried. A new sense of exaltation possessed the country, the exaltation of knowledge and power."[1]

The English mariners sailed all over the world, challenging the monopolies and claims of other countries, trading, raiding and exploring in the Americas. As early as 1527, Robert Thorne of Bristol had said: "There is no land unhabitable, nor sea innavigable."

The English voyagers of the sixteenth century believed that: those words inspired their ventures. They saw new lands, and brought back astonishing tales about the marvels they had seen; and, like the Crusaders before them, they brought back new ideas. In the Indies they saw a tropical profusion of colour: the vivid plumage of strange birds; the flames and jewels of even stranger flowers; glowing insects and queer, armoured reptiles; trees that rose heavenwards like the spires of a city, others whose vast spread of branches would easily shade an entire English village; and over all, thrusting blazing spears down through the leaves, an intense sunlight that swiftly ripened and rotted the plant life of the forest. A whole new world of natural forms and colours was thus revealed to the men who visited the ends of the earth; and their experiences,

[1] *The English Voyages of the Sixteenth Century*, by Sir Walter Raleigh. Written originally as an introduction to the MacLehose Edition of *Hakluyt's Voyages*, 1905.

imparted generation by generation, to their fellow-countrymen, gave the English an unusual appetite for fresh ideas and also gave them a buoyant confidence in the future.

People who could afford to indulge their taste were eager to try out new ideas in the building and equipping of houses. But their eagerness was satisfied by old ideas in a new guise, for ancient Roman architecture now came back to England as the latest Italian fashion. This ready-made architecture had been imposed on the Roman province of Britain fourteen centuries earlier; now it had returned, not as a system introduced by law-giving conquerors and colonisers, but as the most up-to-date form of taste.

The hard-and-fast discipline of Roman architecture, its rigid rules and exact proportions, could not restrain the enthusiasm which the Elizabethans displayed in building. It almost seemed as though the adventurous spirit of the times animated the form of the spacious town and country houses which were built by the nobles and the merchant princes, and all those gay and fearless men who performed acts of towering courage and endurance at sea and who grew rich very quickly and spent their money with a careless magnificance. The country was dominated not only by a new rich class, but by new riches. The simplicity of the early Tudor period, when the spirit of mediaeval building craftsmen was still alive and active, was forgotten; Gothic architecture was dying out. The bold, clean lines of the brick and stone houses that were built in the first quarter of the sixteenth century, were no longer visible; they were hidden beneath tortuous stone fretwork, columns and pilasters—all the standardised features of Roman architecture, which were applied to the outside of houses. But they were only *applied*: they were not an essential part of the process of house building, nor were they willingly adopted by the builders. English craftsmen disliked such foreign fashions: they were out of sympathy with the taste that encouraged them. The foreign models and patterns that carpenters, plasterers and stone-masons were expected to copy, became strange, uncouth and almost monstrous in their practised but unwilling hands. English craftsmen have always shown a sturdy and stubborn liking for their own methods. They probably grumbled vigorously about all the fal-de-rals that were thought of so highly by the nobility and gentry; and a deep, popular contempt existed for the effect of foreign taste upon the well-travelled nobleman. It was said that:

> The Englishman Italianate,
> Is the Devil incarnate.

The way builders copied Italian ideas of decoration, and their mishandling of the Roman orders of architecture, which had come marching back into England after an absence of twelve hundred years, showed that even if they did not actively dislike the forms imposed on them by fashion, they never took the trouble to understand the rules which governed their architectural proportions. The result was that many Elizabethan houses, both inside and out, looked like caricatures of Roman designs. For example, columns were often bloated and bulging, with masses of ornament wrapped round them, or hung on here and there, according to the fancy of the individual. But in spite of all this misunderstanding, architecture showed very vividly the vitality and tireless energy of the Elizabethans.

Many of the country houses built by the merchant class in the previous generation, were enlarged and enriched, redecorated and refurnished, whole new wings and features such as ornamental porches and arcades were added. The last traces of mediaeval lay-out in the arrangement of the house disappeared: buildings were no longer grouped about a courtyard; the shape of the house, as a complete mass of building, was visible to the eye; and for the first time since the days of the castle keep and the watch tower of the fortified manor, country houses were over two storeys in height. Some of the wings rose to four storeys, and beneath the pointed roofs, long, ill-lit attics accommodated servants.

Standing amid formal gardens, these tall country houses in brick and stone, with their array of windows, their arched porches, flanked by columns and carved stonework, seemed to say: "We must be magnificent!" They were certainly in keeping with the energetic and often extravagant life of the country gentry. That period of great and growing prosperity was lit by a passionate love for the arts of life. Men lived with a splendid enthusiasm for the mere act of living. The gaiety of their dress and the range and extent of their accomplishments matched their elaborate surroundings. They conversed and dined and slept in rooms that blazed with colour and gilding, where carved decoration flowed and coiled over walls and furniture, and plaster ceilings were encrusted with moulded strapwork ornament. Those elegant bearded men dressed with a brightness that seemed to have borrowed hues from the tropical forests that so many of them had seen. Their lives were as colourful as their clothes and homes. They pursued wealth and adventure; they were superb soldiers and sailors; they could become, in turn, raiders intent on Spanish loot, explorers seeking fresh trade routes, military leaders helping the Dutch in their fight for independence, courtiers, literary critics, poets, musicians and country gentlemen. Nothing came amiss to them, and in the last third of the sixteenth century they made a revolution in English civilisation, and left a permanent mark upon the character of the English home.

Perhaps that saying, "the good old times", records a memory of the Elizabethan period. People in later ages thought with longing and regret of those spacious days, when the English genius gave so much to the world, when Shakespeare was writing and his plays were being performed, when Englishmen lived a full and stimulating life, and looked with cheerful anticipation to the future. The Elizabethans had neither longing nor regret for the past. The disorders and miseries that had followed the redistribution of power and wealth earlier in the sixteenth century were over: men could enjoy the present and anticipate with high confidence, the future of their country. The home was such an established and well-loved place of cheerfulness, that when in the centuries that followed, right down to our own day, people speak of "the good old times" they are looking back, dimly, to the memory of a time when England, turbulent with enterprise and rich with creative talent, had also mastered the art of home-making.

That highly detailed contemporary record of the home, Harrison's *Description of England*, has nothing but praise for the comforts and conveniences that were enjoyed in Elizabethan England and which were so sharply contrasted with those available in former ages. It also records some of the characteristics of English workmen, and pays a tribute to their skill. "The ancient manours and houses of our gentlemen," writes Harrison, "are yet, and for the most part of strong timber, (in framing whereof our carpenters have been and are worthilie preferred before those of like science among all other nations). Howbeit such as be latelie builded are commonlie either of brick or hard stone (or both); their rooms large and comlie, and houses of office further distant from their lodgings. Those of the nobilitie are likewise wrought with brick and hard stone, as provision may best be made: but so magnificent and statelie, as the basest house of a baron doth often match (in our daies) with some honours of princes in old time. So that if ever curious building did flourish in England, it is in these our years, wherein our workmen excell, and are in manner comparable with skill with old *Vitruvius*, (*Leo Baptisa*), and *Serlo*."[1] Harrison qualifies this compliment by saying that Englishmen charge too much for their work, and that it is cheaper to employ strangers "who are more reasonable in their takings, and less wasters of time by a great deal than our owne".

Of the furnishing of houses, Harrison writes fully and deals with various classes of homes: "I do not speak of the nobilitie and gentrie onlie, but likewise of the lowest sort . . ." The large country house, the small manor, the well-equipped farm, the labourer's cottage— all were improved. They contained more and better furniture; and because the possessions of the rich were overloaded with fashionable ornament, the farmer and the cottager possessed things of greater beauty and actual worth, in terms of sound and simple workman-

[1] *The Description of England*, by William Harrison, Book II, Chap. 12. "Of the manner of building and furniture of our houses."

ELIZABETHAN MANOR HOUSE.

ship, than the owners of the gaudy country houses and the smaller gentry who imitated their luxury. The small homes enjoyed the native architecture and craftsmanship of England; though, as Harrison points out, even the farmer had his share of the luxurious trimmings of life.

In the houses of noblemen it was not rare to see "abundance of Arras, rich hangings of tapestrie, silver vessels, and so much other plate, as may furnish sundrie cupboards, to the summe oftentimes of a thousand or two thousand pounds at the least; whereby the value of this and the rest of their stuffe doth grow to be almost inestimable." In the homes of knights, gentlemen and merchants there was the same lavish display: a "great profusion of tapistrie, Turkey worke, pewter, brass, fine linen, and thereto costly cupboards of plate, worth five or six hundred or a thousand pounds . . ." Such furnishing was no longer confined to the gentry and the merchant class. In Harrison's words: ". . . it is descended yet lower, even unto the inferior artificers and manie farmers, who . . . have . . . learned also to garnish their cupboards with plate, their (joined) beds with tapistrie and silk hangings, and their tables with carpets & fine naperie, whereby the wealth of our countrie (God be praised therefore, and give us grace to imploie it well) doth infinitelie appear. Neither do I speak this in reproach of any man, God is my judge, but to show that I do rejoice rather, to see how God hath blessed us with his good gifts; and whilst I behold how that in a time wherein all things are growen to most excessive prices . . . we do yet find the means to obtain & achieve such furniture as heretofore hath been impossible."

Many examples of this furniture survive to-day, and although the oak stools and tables and cupboards are now darkened by age and generations of polishing, they were once light gold in colour. A golden oak background glowed in the rooms of the large country and town houses, for panelling was used everywhere, and it became increasingly fanciful in design.

In the big country house there would be sitting rooms, a large dining room, many bedrooms, closets and small retiring rooms, and a hall with a great staircase. The kitchen would be the gathering place for the servants, and still a centre of social life for workers on the estate. Where floors were of stone, rushes would be strewn, but oak boards were now used for flooring. Nearly all the furniture would be made of oak, and although the traditional types were still in use, new forms of furniture had been invented. Chests were still common; but they did not always rest directly on the ground; they were often raised on short legs, which formed part of the framing, and their fronts and sides were panelled. The panels were no longer decorated with the linenfold device, but they were frequently carved in the form of round arches, a type of decoration known as arcading.

The horizontal members of panel framing, whether on chests or cupboards or wall panelling, are called rails, and the vertical members are called stiles, and the stiles and rails on chests were often carved with ornament, and mouldings were cut on their edges with a special tool. Sometimes the edges would be smoothed off to make an angle of about 45 degrees between the surface of the stile or rail and the surface of the panel, and this was called chamfering.

Tables gave wood-workers many opportunities for ornamentation; and towards the end of the Elizabethan period they were highly ornamental. Long tables had four, six or eight bulbous legs in the form of Roman columns that had grown fat and mis-shapen. This deformity gave English craftsmen an opportunity for using a lot of what they doubtless called "foreign muckings" by way of decoration. Fashion did not permit these men to do a clean, straightforward job which made the best use of their material, in the manner of their grandfathers and great-grandfathers. Unwillingly "Italianate", they made unwieldy and often ugly furniture, vulgar by reason of its excessive decoration.

Chairs were still rare, though their form was varied. Thomas Wright quotes from inventories of the period to illustrate this scarcity. In 1570, the hall of Bertram Anderson, a wealthy merchant and alderman of Newcastle-on-Tyne, was furnished with "two tables with the carpets (table-covers), three forms, one dozen cushions, half-a-dozen green cushions, one counter with the carpet, two 'basinges' (basins), and two covers, one chair, and one little chair."[1] In the Rectory House of Sedgefield in Durham, "which appears to have been a large house and well entertained," the furniture consisted of "a table of plane-tree with joined frame; two tables of fir with frames, two forms, a settle, and a pair of trestles." No chairs are mentioned, and again, the furnishing of the hall of the manor house of Croxdale, in Durham, in 1571, consisted of "one cupboard, one table, two buffet stools, and one chair; yet Salvin of Croxdale was looked upon as one of the principal gentry . . ."[2]

Chairs were sometimes made of turned spindles, with arms and triangular seats, hard, uncomfortable, but decorative. There were also oak chairs with arms and slightly sloping backs, with carved cresting on the top, and panels in the back, sometimes inlaid with floral patterns in some wood of contrasting colour. On all these hard-seated chairs, loose cushions were used. Another type of chair was designed to suit that large, spreading and unwieldy device, the farthingale; for while Italian fashions were affecting the outside and the inside of the English house, Spanish and French

[1] *A History of Domestic Manners*, by Thomas Wright, Chap. XXI.
[2] *Ibid.*

66

fashions were delighting Elizabethan ladies and irritating English tailors, who saw their customers patronising foreigners.

> "They brought in fashions strange and new with golden garments
>   bright:
> The farthingale, and mighty cuffes, with gownes of rare delight.
> Our London dames in Spanish pride did flourish everywhere."[1]

The farthingale chair had a back but no arms, and it allowed a lady to be seated without disarranging her enormous skirts. Nearly everybody sat on stools. The buffet stools mentioned in the Croxdale inventory are, according to Thomas Wright, "supposed to be the stools with a flat top and a hole in the middle through which the hand might be passed to lift them . . ." The commonest type was the joint or joyned stool. These had four legs, with an underframe tying the feet together close to the ground. They were sometimes known as coffin stools, for two of them could act as supports for a coffin. In taverns, when tempers were lost, these stools were sometimes used as weapons, and many a head was broken with them in a drunken brawl.

There were benches and settles. The latter sometimes had high wooden backs which gave protection from the chill of stone or plaster walls. Some settles had side pieces, which acted as shields against draughts; and this particular type was the forerunner of the wing chair which appeared over a century later.

The beds of the period provided the greatest opportunity for elaboration. They stood like miniature buildings in a room, massive in their architecture, with thick, heavy columns supporting the great roof of a tester. The back or head was lavishly carved with figures flanking arcaded panels; thick, richly embroidered hangings, hung from the tester and slid back and forth on rods which were concealed by an embroidered valance.

Court cupboards, buffets, dressers and side tables accommodated the abundant silver and gold plate that Harrison mentions, and also carried the numerous vessels of pewter that were in use. Spoons and candlesticks were often made of a cheap alloy of brass called latten. Forks were coming into use. Sledge and Meercraft, two characters in Ben Jonson's play, *The Devil is an Ass*, speak of them thus:

> "*Sledge:* Forks! what be they?
> *Meercraft:* The laudable use of forks,
>   Brought into custom here, as they are in Italy,
>   To the sparing of napkins . . ."

Not only were there candlesticks of latten and brass, iron, silver and gold: chandeliers of brass and iron were hung by chains from

---

[1] This verse, from *The Lamentable Fall of Queen Elnor* (Roxburghe Ballads, Vol. II, p. 362), is quoted in Charles W. Camp's book, *The Artisan in Elizabethan Literature*. (Columbia University Press, 1924.)

ELIZABETHAN HOUSES AT SHREWSBURY

These are typical examples of timber-framed buildings in a small town. They vary little, except in ornamental detail, from those built in the fifteenth century.

hooks driven into the wooden beams of ceilings, and half a dozen or more candles would thus shed their light from aloft.

The fire-place was now equipped with tongs and pokers, as well as fire-dogs of ornamental ironwork for supporting logs. The fire-place itself became increasingly important as a feature in a room. The stonework surround was carved with figures and columns; over the fire-place opening a shelf of oak or stone projected into the room, and above that would be an overmantel, either of carved stone or moulded plaster, painted and gilded, or the panelling of the room would be carried across the mantelshelf to form an overmantel, and decorated with architectural features, arcaded panels and carved figures. The fire-place was still a recess in the wall: it was seldom built out into the room, to form what is called a chimney breast.

The windows of most houses were now glazed, and even in town houses of the poorer kind, glass was often used in small panes.

In country houses, sanitation was slightly improved, and Sir John Harrington, a godson of Queen Elizabeth, author, soldier and country gentleman, wrote a book entitled *The Metamorphosis of Ajax*, in which he described a valve water closet which he had invented. He installed this device in his own house at Kelston, but the invention was in advance of its time, and did not have any marked effect on the comfort or hygiene of Elizabethan houses.

But although the Elizabethan house had many drawbacks, compared with a Roman or a modern house, it was a pleasant place, and one foreign observer, Dr. Levinus Lemnius, a Dutch physician, writing at the beginning of the period, records his delighted approval of the Englishman's castle. He said, "the neate cleanlines, the exquisite finenisse, the pleasaunte and delightfull furniture in every poynt for household, wonderfully rejoysed mee; their chambers and parlours strawed over with sweete herbes refreshed me; their nose-gayes finely entermingled wyth sundry sortes of fragruante flours in their bedchambers and privy roomes, with comfortable smell cheered mee up and entirelye delyghted all my senccs." He attri-butes the "incredible curtsie and frendlines of speache and affability used in this famous realme" to the healthful air of England and to good food. "And this do I thinck to be the cause that Englishmen, lyving by such holesome and exquisite meate, and in so holesome and healthfull ayre, be so fresche and cleane coloured; their faces, eyes and countenaunce carying with it and representing a portly grace and comelynes, geveth out evident tokens of an honest mind; in language very smoth and allective, but yet seasoned and tempered within the limits and bonds of moderation, not bumbasted with any unseemly termes, or infarced with any clawing flatteries or allurementes. At their tables, althoughe they be very sumtous, and love to have good fare, yet neyther use they to overcharge themselves with excess of drincke, neyther thereto greatly provoke and urge others, but suffer every man to drincke in such measure as best pleaseth hymself; whych drinck, being eyther Ale or Beere, most pleasaunte in taste and holesomely relised, they fetch not from foreine places, but have it amonge themselves brewed."[1]

Food was abundant, though it was not greatly varied, and cooks certainly had excellent materials. Nobles and wealthy merchants might employ foreign cooks, (whom Harrison describes as "musicall-headed Frenchmen and strangers"[2]), but the farmers, the cottagers and the artisans in the towns still preferred plain dishes. The big kitchen fire became more convenient for the cook. Sometimes brick

[1] Dr. Lemnius wrote in Latin, and a translation first appeared in a book published in London in 1581, entitled *The Touchstone of Complexions*. The extract quoted is included in *England as seen by Foreigners in the days of Elizabeth and James I*, by William Brenchley Rye, published in 1865.

[2] *The Description of England*, by William Harrison, Book II, Chap. VI, "Of the Food and Diet of the English".

or clay ovens were heated by this fire: cooking utensils were more varied and numerous, and the husbandman enjoyed good fare, including beef, pork, mutton, lamb and veal, while for the artisan the town markets provided brawn, pickled pork (which was called souse), bacon, poultry, fruit pies, butter and cheese.[1] "God sends meat, the devil sends cooks" is one of the proverbs included in *Remains Concerning Britain*, a book written by William Camden, the historian and antiquary, who was born in 1551. It is possible that the nobility and gentry, when they employed foreign cooks, were not only indulging their taste for extravagance and elaboration.

There was but little difference between the large country or town house; they enjoyed the same luxurious diversity of equipment; their rooms were spacious; and they were built of the best materials that money could buy. But the largest of them were built wastefully; they were casually planned; their enormous rooms, linked by long corridors, were inconvenient, and, because of their lavish decoration, unrestful. Thomas Gray, writing in the eighteenth century, an age when good planning was widely appreciated, criticised those Elizabethan houses in the opening verses of a poem entitled *A Long Story*.

"In Britain's isle, no matter where,
    An ancient pile of building stands:
The Huntingdons and Hattons there
    Employed the power of fairy hands
"To raise the ceiling's fretted height,
    Each panel in achievements clothing,
Rich windows that exclude the light,
    And passages, that led to nothing."

Rich London merchants now built their houses in the city suburbs, within easy reach of their offices and warehouses. The rapid growth of London beyond the walls alarmed the government, and in 1580 a proclamation was issued by Queen Elizabeth. This described the congestion and the unwholesome housing conditions with brutal frankness. The small house in the town was now far inferior to the cottage. In the country the lot of the cottager had improved beyond anything known or even imagined in previous ages. But in the towns few changes had occurred. The artisans and small tradesmen had more possessions, but that was all. The houses they lived in were often two or three centuries old. Elizabethan London was still the timber and plaster city it had been when Henry VII was crowned. New, grand houses had been built here and there; additions had been made to some of the palaces; the great spire of St. Paul's Cathedral, once among the highest in Europe, had been destroyed by lightning in 1561; but there was no substantial change,

[1] *The Description of England*, by William Harrison, Book II, Chap. VI, "Of the Food and Diet of the English".

EARLY SEVENTEENTH-CENTURY BED

The oak panelled back and the turned posts support a heavy, panelled oak tester.

and a Londoner of the fourteenth or fifteenth century could have found his way about easily, for many familiar landmarks remained, and he would have recognised many houses as old friends.

The Queen's proclamation stated bluntly that the health of the increasing population was in danger "where there are such great multitudes of people brought to inhabit in small rooms, whereof a great part are seen very poor, yea, such as must live of begging, or by worse means, and they heaped up together, and in a sort smothered by many families of children and servants in one house or small tenement; it must needs follow, if any plague or popular sickness should, by God's permission, enter amongst those multitudes, that the same would not only spread itself, and invade the whole city and confines, but that a great mortality would ensue . . . the infection would be also dispersed through all other parts of the realm, to the manifest danger of the whole body thereof . . ." (Three quarters of a century later, the plague came, and ravaged the city and the country as Elizabeth had foreseen.) The proclamation charged and strictly commanded "all manner of persons, of what quality soever they be, to desist and forbear from any new buildings of any house or tenement within three miles from any of the gates of the city of London, to serve for habitation of lodging for any person, where no former house hath been known to have been in the memory of such as are now living; and also to forbear from letting or setting, or suffering any more families than one only to be placed, or to inhabit from henceforth, in any house that heretofore hath been inhabited."

This proclamation, which announced severe penalties for disobedience, became an Act of Parliament in 1592. It was an attack on overcrowding, and its aim, a private house for every family, was excellent: unfortunately it did not consider the possibility of planning the growth of the town in advance, so that it could expand tidily and healthfully. Sir Thomas More's spacious city of Amaurote was still a dream, and London continued to grow untidily, for the laws against new building were evaded. From the end of the sixteenth century to the beginning of the Second World War, English cities steadily devoured the countryside that surrounded them.

But in Elizabeth's reign there were still many acres of uncultivated land, great tracts of forest, a huge area of undrained fenland in Norfolk and Lincoln. The countryside was not yet seriously threatened by invasion from the towns. In the course of the sixteenth century that countryside had been enriched by the introduction of the holm oak, the plane tree and the common spruce. It was a deeply peaceful, prosperous and beautiful land; and the English home at its best was to be found in cottage and farmhouse, manor and mansion, and the uncrowded houses of small towns.

SIXTEENTH CENTURY LONDON STREET WITH HALF-TIMBERED BUILDINGS.

CHAPTER VIII

EARLY STUART HOUSES
(A.D. 1603–1640)

IR HENRY WOTTON, author, poet and diplomatist, published a book in 1624 called *The Elements of Architecture*. Based on the writings of Vitruvius, it was the English interpretation of those Roman rules and regulations that had cramped English builders and worried craftsmen for over a hundred years. It contained a sentence which has since been widely quoted: "Well-building hath three conditions, Commodity, Firmness and Delight." During the seventeenth century those three conditions were honoured by English builders; and in the making of homes, large or small, they made *privacy* another condition of "well-building".

Sir Edward Coke, that great upholder of the common law, who was Elizabeth's attorney general and Chief Justice under James I, had said: "The house of every one is to him as his castle and fortress, as well for his defence against injury and violence as for his repose." Queen Elizabeth's proclamation about the growth of London had underlined the importance of privacy: one house for every family. Her words gave official recognition to a deep-rooted national characteristic. No good architect ever forgot to safeguard the privacy of the English householder; and after the end of the Elizabethan period, the architect gradually became the most important influence in the building of large or small houses, although only a few houses were actually designed by architects.

It was one of the architect's tasks to bring order out of the chaos caused by the foreign fashions that had crowded their way into England and English heads for over a century. The early Stuart house was burdened with the excesses of luxury: the shape of everything in the homes of the rich was complicated by a vulgar profusion of carving and embellishment. Everything was overdone. Clothes, furniture and interior decoration were gross in their extravagance; wood, plaster and stone were tortured into forms that were loutish and coarse. Elizabethan houses in country and town, had certainly displayed increasing elaboration; but the Elizabethans possessed great vitality; all their versions of Italian ornament, although blunted by the obstructiveness of English workmen, were at least alive. But in the reign of James I, the Jacobean period as it was called, everything became heavy and drowsy, and drooped with masses of ornament. It seemed as though the taste of the nobility and gentry had thickened.

Meanwhile the printing presses of Amsterdam were turning

out hundreds of copy books for the use of builders, copiously illustrated by engraved plates of the orders of architecture with variations and ornamental odds and ends calculated to appeal to men who wanted to display their wealth everywhere. These copy books, imported from Holland, helped to spread the fashions that were in favour at the court of James I. The confusion of the English builder and craftsman was increased by such means, and the art of building might have suffered severely if the influence of James's court had been as great as that of Elizabeth's; but it was a corrupt and degenerate court, which commanded no respect outside the fashionable circle of noblemen, and the artists and writers and players who provided entertainment. The life of the country gentry was independent of the tastes and amusements of that little gay world. But it was from the court that a new, refining and simplifying influence in architecture emerged.

On Twelfth Night, 1604–1605, a Masque, entitled "The Masque of Blacknesse" was performed before the court at Whitehall, and the setting and scenery "was of Master Inigo Jones' design and act."[1] The name of this designer, at first heard only in connection with the court masques written by Ben Jonson, was to become the most famous in the history of English building. He was the son of a London cloth-worker, and was born in 1573. The form and character of English houses were powerfully influenced by his ideas, not only during his lifetime, but for over a hundred and fifty years after his death.

In the latter part of Elizabeth's reign, an architect named John Thorpe had built great houses in the Italian manner. Kirby Hall, Northamptonshire, is an example of his work; and its elaborate entrance has been described as "a riot of useless columns . . ."[2] Thorpe was an inventive architect: Inigo Jones was a genius, and as such his name resounds in the history of English architecture, and to this day the mark of his creative mind remains, and affects the external appearance and internal arrangement of houses in the mid-twentieth century.

Little is known of his early life; but he studied architecture in Italy, and he understood how to use with imagination the great system of design that governs the Roman orders and regulates their proportions. Twice had that system of design entered the country with paralysing effect; twice had it stunted native talent for building. At last an Englishman had learnt how to use it as a master and not as a slave.

The architecture of Inigo Jones had life and liberty of a kind that was unknown in the Roman Empire where its forms had originated. He built houses which were as English in character as

[1] *Some Architectural Works of Inigo Jones*, by H. Inigo Triggs and Henry Tanner, Jn.
[2] *The History of the English House*, by Nathaniel Lloyd, Chap. V, p. 63.

TILE-HUNG HOUSES IN A SMALL SUSSEX TOWN

Built in the early seventeenth century, these houses had tiles hung on the
upper storey. Nearly every county had its own characteristic methods of using
local materials.

the early Tudor houses, though different in form and appearance.
He worked out their proportions, so that the last traces of muddle
and haphazard growth disappeared, and a new, orderly, well-
balanced type of building smiled graciously upon the formal gardens
that surrounded it, if it stood in the country, or gave dignity to
some street, if it adorned a town. He did not build very many
houses, and although he designed the great palace of Whitehall,
which would have been the wonder of Europe had it ever been
completed, he only built a small fragment of it, the Banqueting Hall,
which still survives. Among the few great country houses he
designed are Lees Court, Faversham; Raynham Hall in Norfolk ;
and, most famous of all, Wilton House in Wiltshire. In 1610 he
was appointed Surveyor to Henry, Prince of Wales, and in 1614
he became Surveyor of the Works to James I, and he remained in
the Royal service until Charles I was beheaded. It has been suggested
that he re-conditioned and largely rebuilt Ham House, at Petersham
on the Thames, not far from the old Royal Palace of Richmond,
for Prince Henry; in appearance that house certainly suggests that
it was built by an architect with a new understanding of design.
Inigo Jones *planned* his houses as a whole; and although Thorpe
in the previous century, had planned symmetrical houses, sometimes
in the form of the letter H, and sometimes with a fancifulness which

seldom reached the stage of actual building, a plan by Inigo Jones decided the whole character of a house. The size, shape and disposition of the rooms, their relationship to each other, and the arrangement of windows, doorways, chimney stacks and every external feature, were under control; there were no after-thoughts to disturb the orderly lay-out that had been planned with such disciplined imagination. With the example of such tidy and beautifully proportioned buildings to guide them, architects could no longer tolerate a casual collection of rooms and architectural features, jumbled together anyhow; they could not allow windows to sprawl over the front of the house, or wings to bud off here and there, or some pretentious porch to flaunt its fussy columns and ornamentation, and so draw attention to itself at the expense of everything else, so that the house appeared to be a mere attachment to this extravagant and often unnecessary feature. The smaller country houses, and the larger farmhouses had never been troubled by the Italianate complexities that appealed to the gentry. Those comfortable homes were the work of country builders, glad of the chance to do a straightforward job; the Gothic tradition was still alive in their hands, and it remained alive in remote districts throughout the seventeenth century, surviving in modified forms in some parts of the west country and East Anglia until the First World War. Some Cotswold builders would, up to a few years ago, build windows and fireplaces in stone just as they were built in the reign of Henry VII. They were not copied from models; that way of building had been handed down from father to son for generations in a family business.

But in due time the effect of Inigo Jones's work left its mark on the towns and country houses of England. Outside they gained new dignity from the proportions of classic architecture, and from tall, rectangular windows, which were divided vertically by one mullion, of wood or stone, and horizontally by a transome, placed at about three-quarters of the height of the window opening. Glazing bars of lead or iron, enclosed small square or rectangular panes. This new arrangement of window panes, and the disappearance of close-set mullions, gave more light to rooms and made the windows into a regular pattern on the outside. The early Tudor and many of the Elizabethan houses had presented great masses of stone-framed glass to the eye; but now the windows were drawn up in ranks on each floor. Sometimes a window would have a semi-circular head; particularly when it occupied a central position and lit a staircase or a hall. Later in the seventeenth century the sliding sash window replaced the casement; and the windows of an Inigo Jones house prepared a handsome stone frame for the sash.[1]

[1] Raymond McGrath and A. C. Frost suggest that some form of sash window was used early in the sixteenth century, though the first recorded use of the balanced sliding sash in England was in 1685. *Glass in Architecture and Decoration*, Section II, p. 97.

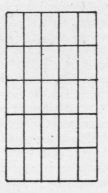

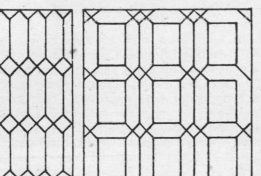
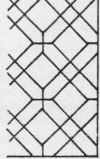

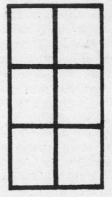

METHODS OF GLAZING

Above: early sixteenth century. *Centre:* mid-sixteenth and early seventeenth century. *Below, left:* late sixteenth and early seventeenth century. *Below, right:* late seventeenth century.

Apart from the example set by these new houses, and the new skill and thought they represented, a most important change took place in the principal materials used for building. In 1625 the sizes of bricks were regulated by statute, and the sizes used to-day, 9 in. by 4½ in. by 3 in., were adopted as a general standard. Before that, bricks had been small, not unlike tiles, and had varied enormously in size, each brickworks having its own ideas about shape and dimensions; so brick buildings differed in character in each brickmaking locality. The establishment of a standard unit, although it was not accepted in every part of the country, did simplify the business of building; and it became easier for local builders to follow the proportions that architects laid down. Standardisation is sometimes thought of as the monotonous repetition of set and unchanging forms and shapes; but standardised units, such as bricks, window frames, doors, and so forth, are a great convenience to builders, and they may be used in a great variety of ways to suit the needs of different house plans.

The interior of the large country or town house also gained much from the work of Inigo Jones. Chimney-pieces, ceilings, panelling, the frames surrounding doors and windows (which are called architraves), cornices and friezes, were still richly carved and moulded; but their proportions were improved. The decoration was no longer loaded with lavish carelessness upon a surface; it was used to emphasise the constructional lines of a feature. These improvements did not spread rapidly all over the country. They were only adopted gradually, and the mischief done by the foreign copy books remained. The design of furniture, for instance, was not affected by the new understanding of good proportion. Most of the larger articles, the court cupboards and buffets, the long, bulbous-legged tables, the overpowering beds, still writhed and bulged with misplaced embellishment. But some notable inventions were made. The gate-leg table first appeared in the Jacobean period, and although it was not fully developed until the middle of the seventeenth century, the principle of a swinging leg to support a hinged flap was used on a few small tables. Great improvements were made in chair design. Upholstery was invented, and the chair with a cushion permanently attached to its framework, became a familiar article in the furnishing of the more luxurious country and town houses. These stuffed chairs, with their seats heavily padded with horsehair or wool, were covered with rich fabrics; often their seats and backs would display elaborate needlework, and they would be trimmed with tasselled fringes, which hung down like skirts from the lower part of the seat cushion, dangling over the under-framing. Some richly upholstered experiments were also worked out with X-shaped chairs. The X-frame had been developed in the late Middle Ages, but it was not until the seventeenth century

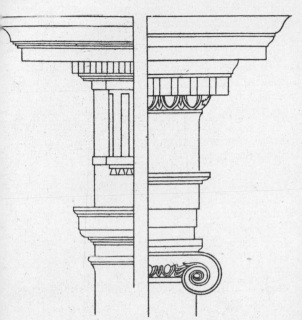

THE ROMAN ORDERS

During the sixteenth century the Roman Orders came marching back into the country, but their proportions were misunderstood and mismanaged until, early in the seventeenth century, Inigo Jones mastered them, and made them serve English architecture.

that its possibilities were fully realised, and the strong, curved framework was close-covered in damask, a large embroidered cushion was set loose in the cupped seat, the back was padded, and decorated by two little knobs or finials which gave the chair a regal appearance.

Carpets, which in the past had been used chiefly for spreading on the lids of chests or on table-tops, were now sometimes used on the polished, wooden floors of rooms. Stone floors would still be strewn with rushes, and many years were to pass before floors were really clean.

Pictures thronged the panelled walls, and many houses had long galleries in which the space between the dado and the frieze would be covered with patterned fabric, to form a background for paintings. All kinds of luxury goods were imported from overseas, and curious carvings, pieces of classical sculpture from Italy, exotic jars and bowls from the East, and innumerable objects, useless, ornamental, costly, elegant or cumbersome, according to the good taste or collecting mania of the owner, found a place on some shelf or side table. Sometimes all this decorative diversity was reflected by mirrors, small, dark, and with a curious depth of blue in them; but their dimensions were as yet restricted, because the art of glass-making was still limited in its possibilities in England. But mirrors, as well as glass vessels, were imported from Venice. "The earliest English factory for the making of looking-glass plates was set up in the reign of James I by Sir Robert Mansell, who imported Venetian workmen for the instruction of the English, but prior to the reign of Charles II English mirrors were small in size and mainly utilized as dressing-glasses, larger mirrors to hang on walls being mostly of Venetian manufacture."[1]

Walls were not always panelled or covered with pictures: tapestry was still used, and in 1619, Sir Francis Crane, under the patronage of the King, established the famous works at Mortlake, where Dr. Dee, Queen Elizabeth's astrologer had lived. For over half a century Mortlake tapestries were celebrated for their excellence, but the industry did not survive, although the use of decorative fabrics of all kinds increased during the seventeenth century.

The fire-place was the chief feature in most rooms, and the focal point of comfort in winter. Dogs in cast iron sometimes supported a basket which confined the logs or coals, and raised the fire above the level of the hearth. The dog grate was thus evolved, and this tidying up of the fireplace interior destroyed the old-fashioned, sprawling friendliness of the open fire, which survived only in the farmhouse and the cottage. Cast iron firebacks, with heraldic devices and other ornamental patterns, had come into use, and they glowed at the back of the fireplace, shiny black against the sooty brick or stone interior.

In the kitchen, the range had appeared.

"A boiler, range, and dresser were the fountains
    Of all the knowledge in the universe . . ."

Those lines are spoken by Lickfinger, a character in Ben Jonson's play, *The Staple of News*. The long cooking stove with its confined fire, its ovens and racks, was by no means the compact and convenient appliance that it became in a later age; and in the farmhouse, while ovens might flank the kitchen fire, the fire itself was still unenclosed and cheerfully ravenous for fuel. Cooking utensils had increased in variety and efficiency. Tall oak dressers with shelves for crockery and drawers for knives and forks and spoons made good use of wall space.

[1] *Glass in Architecture and Decoration*, by Raymond McGrath and A. C. Frost. Section III, p. 311.

COUNTRY HOUSE OF THE TYPE DESIGNED BY INIGO JONES : SASH WINDOWS
WOULD BE ADDED LATER.

In the country, more and better cottages were built. New fortunes were being made from overseas trade; the founding of the East India Company and the development of the Virginian colony brought money to London and other cities, and the successful trader generally wanted to leave the town and settle down as a country squire. New estates were planned, and the new landowners built cottages of brick or stone for their labourers and dependents. They often had glass in the windows, and roofs of tile or slate instead of thatch. It was not considered odd or extravagant to build cottages of permanent materials: landlords no longer thought of their tenants' dwellings as temporary shells, makeshift and perishable. That mediaeval way of thinking had arisen, not from the landlord's selfish disregard for the welfare of his dependents, for he was their lord and directly responsible for their well-being, but because in the old lawless days of private warfare, cottages were always destroyed when a castle was beseiged, and it was waste of time and material to make them permanent. But in the new, enlarged world of the seventeenth century, the Middle Ages were far off, and mediaeval ways of thought and habits had faded from life, save in a few remote country districts.

"A much larger area came under the control of landowners who were receptive to new ideas and who had the capital to indulge them. The growth of farming as a great national concern is distinctly marked during these years of transition and change, and by nothing more clearly than by the readjustment of the balance between the production of wool and of corn which . . . had become rather badly disturbed in Tudor times."[1]

While the countryman flourished, the towns grew more congested. Royal proclamations could not check the growth of London; and builders ignored those issued in 1604 and 1607, forbidding new building within the city, and commanding that any legal new building should be faced with brick or stone. Timber was becoming scarce; it was needed for ship-building. Some new trees had been introduced, notably the horse chestnut and the silver fir. But there was no afforestation plan to restore the denuded woodlands. In Howe's second edition of Stow's *Annales*, published in 1631, it is stated that: "Such hath been the plenty of wood in England for all uses, that, within man's memory, it was held impossible to have any want of wood in England; but contrary to former imaginations, such hath beene the great expence of timber for Navigation, with infinite increase of building of houses, with the great expence of wood to make household furniture, caskes, and other vessels not to be numbered, and of Carts, Wagons, and Coaches, besides the extreame wast of Wood in making Iron, burning of brick and tile, That

---

[1] *The Englishman's Food: A History of Five Centuries of English Diet*, by J. C. Drummond and Anne Wilbraham. Chap. V, Section 1, "Rise of the Great Estates", p. 111.

HOUSES AT CHIPPING CAMPDEN

Half-timbered houses, with stone work on the ground floor, adjoin houses
built completely in stone (see also page 142).

whereas in the yeere of our Lord God, 1306, King Edward the
first, by proclamation prohibited the burning of Sea coale in London
and the Suburbs, to avoid the sulferous smoke and savour of that
firing; and in the same proclamation commanded all persons, to
make their fires of wood, which was performed by all, (Smiths
onely excepted), yet at this present, through the great consuming
of wood as aforesaid, and the neglect of planting of woods, there is
so great scarcitie of wood through-out the whole kingdom, that
not only the Cittie of London, all haven towns, and in very many
parts within the Land the inhabitants in generall are constrained
to make their fiers of Sea coale or pit coale, even in the Chambers of
honourable personages. And through necessitie, which is the mother
of all artes, they have of very late yeares devised the making of
Iron, the making of all sorts of glasse and burning of bricke, with
Sea coale or pit coale."

The atmosphere of towns and cities, and especially of London,
grew foul. The grandeur and size of a few new buildings marked
the only architectural changes that had taken place in London
for generations. As the countryside grew richer and the welfare of
the countryman increased, the artisans and prentice boys and small
tradesmen lived in tall, overcrowded and often tottering houses,
lining streets through which filth flowed in open kennels, while
overhead a smoke cloud, fed by thousands of chimneys, grew a
little larger and darker every year, and on still days in autumn and
winter it descended, mingled with the river mists, and filled the
streets with acrid, impenetrable fog. The brightly coloured city,
still largely mediaeval in appearance, was growing a little tarnished.
By modern standards, most of the small houses in it would have
been condemned as unfit for human habitation.

CHAPTER IX

THE PURITAN HOME
(A.D. 1640-1660)

ENGLAND passed through a political and cultural revolution in the middle years of the seventeenth century. The Puritans during the Commonwealth gained control of the country and they interfered with the life of the people to an intolerable extent. Despite all their great qualities, their courage and their resistance to tyranny, they became relentless tyrants themselves when they assumed the responsiblity for governing England. They ignored the English love of liberty and diversity; the officers of the Puritan government enquired into the private lives of anybody who was suspected of critical thinking. Privacy was at an end: the door of the Englishman's castle no longer protected him, for any prying state official could enter and question everybody in the household, and make his report to fanatics whose powers of interference and persecution were unbounded. So many new sins were invented that ordinary people never knew where they stood with the law. Christmas could no longer be celebrated. Mince-pies were sinful; plum pudding was banned; the theatre was a form of criminal activity; the sports and pastimes of the people were frowned on and ruthlessly regulated, and that ancient English festival on May Day, when villagers and townsmen too, danced round the Maypole, was strictly forbidden. Practically everything that contributed to the ease and cheerfulness of life was banned.

English gentlemen who could afford to do so, spent much of their time abroad to escape the growing gloom; but in town and country the people had to endure the rule of stern, pleasure-hating soldiers and officials. But even the exiles returned after a time: the new state of affairs seemed to be established, the King had been executed, and Cromwell and his roundheads were firmly in the saddle. That observant gentleman, John Evelyn, explains in his *Diary* his reason for coming back to England in 1652. In the entry for March 9, he wrote: "I went to Deptford, where I made preparation for my settlement, no more intending to go out of England, but endeavour a settl'd life, either in this or some other place, there being now so little appearance of any change for the better, all being entirely in the Rebells hands . . ."

For the next few years Evelyn's *Diary* records the sort of life a cultivated gentleman could lead in Puritan England. Here and there he gives glimpses of well-ordered homes, of the occasional introduction of new foreign ideas by travelled gentlemen, of the devas-

MID-SEVENTEENTH-CENTURY INTERIOR

Puritan severity was reflected in the lines of furniture: carved ornament was
limited: chairs were upholstered in leather instead of rich fabrics; fringes and
tasselled trimming were banned.

tation wrought by the Puritans. He orders a coach for his wife "the pattern whereof I had brought out of Paris" (April 29, 1652). He is robbed on the way from Tunbridge Wells to London, within three miles of Bromley, by "two cut-throates", and the richness of dress affected by gentlemen of the period is revealed by his description of the robbery. "What they got of money was not considerable, but they took two rings, the one an emerald with diamonds, the other an onyx, and a pair of bouckles set with rubies and diamonds . . ." (June 11, 1652.) He was passionately interested in houses and gardens. He frequently refers to the importance attached to the partnership between a country house and its surroundings; for the laying out of parks and gardens and the deliberate choosing of prospects had become a part of architecture. He visits his neighbour, Sir Henry Newton at Charlton, and considered "the prospect, which is doubtless for city, river, ships, medows, hill, woods, and all other amenities, one of the most noble in the world; so as had the house running water, it were a princely seat." (June 9, 1653.) He goes to Hackney "to see my Lady Brook's garden, which was one of the neatest and most celebrated in England, the house well furnish'd, but a despicable building. Returning, visited one Mr. Tombs's garden; it has large and noble walks, some modern statues, a vineyard, planted in strawberry borders, staked at 10 foote distances; the banquetting-house of cedar, where the couch and scates were carv'd *a l'antique*; some good pictures in the house, especialy one of Vandyke's, being a *Man in his shirt*; also some of Stenwyck. I also call'd at Mr. Ducie's who has indeede a rare collection of the best masters, and one of the largest stories of H. Holbein. I also saw Sir Tho. Fowler's aviarie, which is a poore businesse." (May 8, 1654.) He refers to a house at Aldermaston, the property of Sir Humphry Forster, "built *a la moderne*".

He travelled a lot in 1654, and visited Bath, which was "intirely built of stone, but the streets narrow, uneven, and unpleasant." At Oxford he visited "that miracle of a youth Mr. Christopher Wren, nephew of the Bishop of Ely." He saw Lord Craven's house at Caversham "now in ruines, his goodly woods felling by the Rebells." He found Sir John Glanvill, formerly Speaker of the House of Commons, living in the gate-house of his estate at Broad-Hinton, "his very faire dwelling-house having ben burnt by his owne hands to prevent the rebells making a garrison of it." Here he was shown "such a lock for a doore, that for its filing and rare contrivances was a master-piece, yet made by a country black-smith. But we have seene watches made by another with as much curiositie as the best of that profession can brag of; and not many yeares after, there was nothing more frequent than all sorts of Iron-work more exquisitely wrought and polish'd than in any part of Europ,

HOUSE AT FLADBURY, WORCESTERSHIRE

Many English houses have grown from one century to another: a seventeenth century core with later additions, and tidy, Georgian windows can create a comfortable home.

so as a dore-lock of a tolerable price was esteen'd a curiositie even among forraine princes."

This is an interesting side-light on the inventive skill of English craftsmen, who were turning their thoughts to mechanical contrivances, and were soon to become great clock-makers.

He gives us a picture of Salisbury, then, as now, a small city, little more than a market town. "The merket place with most of the streetes are watere'd by a quick current and pure streame running thro' the middle of them, but are negligently kept, when with small charge they might be purg'd and render'd infinitely agreeable,

and made one of the sweetest townes, but now the common buildings are despicable and the streetes are dirty."

He is constantly remarking upon modern houses, the new houses
that were showing signs of the new understanding of planning and
architectural design. Evelyn was himself a shrewd critic of architecture. An early entry in the *Diary* (February 26, 1649) shows how
educated gentlemen had rebelled against the coarseness and heavi-
ness of Jacobean buildings. "Came to see me Capt. Geo. Evelyn
my kinsman, the greate traveller, and one who believed himself a
better architect than really he was, witness the Portico in the garden
at Wotton; yet the greate roome at Albury is somewhat better
understood. He had a large mind, but he overbuilt every thing."

The work of Inigo Jones had ended the period when architects
and their patrons "overbuilt everything", and the reign of the
Puritans arrested the extravagant architectural development of the
country houses. For a few years the Englishman's castle became a
sombre and sober-minded place. Inside, all frills and trimmings
were banished from furniture; carved ornament was restricted on
woodwork; the legs of chairs were plainly turned and leather seats
and backs replaced the rich fabrics and their fringes and tassels.
The nobility and gentry became nervous of excessive display.
English craftsmen were released from any need to follow foreign
fashions. But a few foreign fashions entered some parts of the
country. For example, when the Norfolk and Cambridgeshire fens
were drained under the direction of the Dutch engineer, Cornelius
Vermuyden, who was knighted by Charles I, many Dutch settlers
came to the reclaimed lands, and built houses and villages. The old
marshland between Downham and Wisbech is like Holland in its
scenery and architecture. The Dutch influence can be seen in many
buildings—in the rounded gables, in the dolls'-house neatness—and is
preserved in local place-names, such as the village of Nordelph.
Here and there, particularly in those parts of the country where
stone was used, in the Cotswolds, in Yorkshire, the Mendips and
Cornwall, old, sturdy Gothic forms once more appeared. With
centuries of accumulated skill, with a larger range of materials to
work with, better tools and a new freedom for using them, wood-
workers, masons and smiths began to build and equip houses as
truly English in character as those of Early Tudor times.

Such conveniences as the gate-leg table were more widely adopted.
Brass "bird-cage" or "lantern" clocks were made, and they stood on
brackets fixed high on the wall, to give room to the weights and
long pendulum. A new form of chest appeared, which had a deep
base with a couple of drawers in it. It was halfway between the old
chest with a lid, and the chest of drawers which was made later on
in the seventeenth century, and it was called a mule chest. In woodwork, there was a great development of turning. The legs of chairs

COTTAGES AT RICHMOND, YORKSHIRE

Domestic building in the seventeenth century became immensely varied, but even in the smallest houses privacy was guarded.

were turned in many decorative patterns, and the twisted leg was invented. The old, human desire for ornament could not be wholly repressed, even by the Puritans, and although carved decoration almost disappeared, decorative twisting and turning took its place. Legs were turned with bobbins on them, and the twist known as the barley-sugar twist became popular.

The period had a good effect upon the design of houses. It cleared away a lot of rubbish in the shape of badly executed ornament, and it abolished many of the clumsy, ugly shapes that had overpowered the rooms of large town and country houses. It enabled the work of Inigo Jones to be followed by other architects, and while that father of English architecture was being persecuted by the Puritans, other men were learning by his example.

Although building still continued in the country, and the reclaiming of large tracts of the Lincolnshire, Norfolk and Cambridge fens enriched those eastern counties and caused towns to be extended and new villages to be built, there was little improvement in the small town house. Evelyn mentions the laying out of a long street in Hatton Garden, "design'd for a little towne, lately an ample garden", during one of his visits to London (June 7, 1659); but there was no change in the overcrowded housing conditions that had worried Queen Elizabeth and her councillors. If Evelyn had a poor opinion of Bath and Salisbury, he was even more critical of "the old and ragged Citty of Leicester, large and pleasantly seated, but despicably built, the chimney flues like so many smiths' forges . . ."

Those smoking chimneys were typical of English cities and towns, large or small. Sea-coal filled the grates that had now been raised well above the hearth level. The fire basket was sometimes a fixture in the kitchen, and consisted of bars built between stone or brick hobs. Ovens with cast iron doors were often built into these hobs. Inventive gentlemen like Sir John Winter, might attempt to popularise a form of coke, so that coals could "make a cleare pleasant chamber fire, depriv'd of their sulphur and arsenic malignity"[1]; but the glowing comfort of a coal fire was too pleasant for most people to bother about the smoke it made. In farmhouse and cottage, the huge fireplace was really an alcove in the living room, with seats or high-backed settles on either side, but in those fireplaces wood was burned, and the chimney mouth would be used for curing bacon in the woodsmoke. The "chimney corner" was the most sociable, comfortable place in the small house.

Hearth and home have always been closely connected in the minds of Englishmen; and even the Puritans did not attempt to disturb or forbid the lighting and enjoyment of fires.

[1] Evelyn's *Diary*, July 11, 1656.

CHAPTER X

THE GOLDEN AGE OF BUILDING BEGINS
(A.D. 1660–1680)

CHARLES II was a man of educated taste. Like his father and grandfather, he had his taste in architecture guided by a man of genius. James I and Charles I were the patrons of Inigo Jones; in 1661 Charles II appointed a young, imaginative professor of astronomy as Assistant to the Surveyor General. That young professor was Christopher Wren. A modern writer on architecture has suggested that "If an analogy from the Scriptures is allowed it might be said that 'Inigo Jones planted, whilst Sir Christopher watered'."[1]

Five years after his appointment Wren was given the greatest opportunity that any architect ever had, for London was burnt down and he had the chance of planning a new city to replace the ruins. He made the plan, but the seventeenth-century Londoners missed the opportunity. Property owners and their lawyers made the adoption of a new street plan impossible, so the maze of mediaeval streets remained, with residential and industrial quarters mixed up and industry continually seeking fresh expansion. A year before the fire, the pestilence that Queen Elizabeth had dreaded smote the city: it had a greater area to ravage than existed in her reign, for London had continued to grow under its smoke cloud. That cloud was fed chiefly by the prosperous industrial enterprises, for the householders' contribution in the way of smoke was only considerable in the winter. John Evelyn saw very clearly that smoke-producing industries should not be allowed in the city. He wrote a pamphlet in 1661, which he addressed to the new King, and entitled it: *Fumifugium, or the Inconvenience of the Aer and the Smoake of London Dissipated*.[2] He briefly examined the possibility of returning to wood fuel; but he realised that this could not cure the trouble. "That to talk of serving this vast City (though *Paris* as great, be so supplied) with *Wood*, were madnesse; and yet doubtless it were possible, that much larger proportions of Wood might be brought to *London*, and sold at easier rates, if that were diligently observed, which both our *Laws* enjoyn, as faisible and practised in other places more remote, by Planting and preserving of *Woods* and *Copses*, and by what might by Sea, be brought out of the *Northern Countries*, where it so greatly abounds, and seems inexhaustible. But the

[1] *Inigo Jones*, by Stanley C. Ramsey, ("Masters of Architecture" series), p. 23.
[2] Reprinted by the National Smoke Abatement Society, with an introduction by Rose Macaulay, in 1933.

Remedy which I would propose, has nothing in it of this difficulty, requiring only the Removal of such *Trades*, as are manifest *Nuisances* to the City, which, I would have placed at farther distances; especially, such as in their Works and Fournaces use great quantities of *Sea-Coale*, the sole and only cause of those prodigious Clouds of *Smoake*, which so universally and so fatally infest the *Aer*, and would in no City of *Europe* be permitted, where Men had either respect to Health or Ornament. Such we named to be *Brewers, Diers, Sope* and *Salt-boylers, Lime-burners*, and the like: These I affirm, together with some few others of the same Classe removed at competent distance, would produce so considerable (though but partial), a Cure, as Men would even be found to breath a new life as it were, as well as *London* appear a new City . . ."

Chimneys did receive some official recognition; but not as public nuisances. In the same year that Evelyn wrote *Fumifugium*, a tax was levied on them at the rate of 2s. per annum on each chimney.[1] It did not last long enough to affect the design of houses, for in 1666 property owners were allowed to free their houses from this tax at eight years' purchase. (This raised £1,600,000 to meet a sum voted by Parliament for the King's use.)

The smoke canopy overhead was not the chief cause of ill health in London. Although, as Mr. Arthur Bryant has written, "the country's capital was still rural at heart, and the rich earth smell of the fruits and beasts of the home counties lay about it," there were other smells.[2] "The sanitation of the day was Oriental in its simple grandeur, and its effects, comparatively innocuous in a country village, were appallingly noticeable in the metropolis. Rivers of filth coursed down the centre of each street, and at the time of the emptying of slop-pails, the passer-by nearest the wall had cause to be grateful for the overhanging stories. Around the city stretched a halo of stinking, steaming lay-stalls, haunted by flies and kites, while in the densest quarters of the city the graveyards, piled high above the surrounding ground, re-peopled themselves. Even on a spring evening, when the air was full of scents of sap and blossom from the trees that shaded every court and alley garden, the citizen taking the air on the leads of his house was sometimes driven indoors . . ."[3] As Mr. Bryant points out, "the most cultured, however nice in their own tastes, were utterly innocent of public sanitary sense . . ."

This pestilential and congested city of wood and plaster was swept away by the great fire. Sir Thomas More's dream city nearly came to life. London might have been in reality "commodious and handsome" with "houses of fair and gorgeous building"—it

[1] Pepys mentions the tax on March 3, 1661, in his *Diary*, and again during October 15 and 18, 1666.
[2] *The England of Charles II*, by Arthur Bryant, Chap. II, p. 16.   [3] *Ibid.*

COTTAGE IN DEVONSHIRE

Thatched roof and walls of plastered brickwork, colour-washed in pink, cream or white, are typical of cottages and small houses in this county. The type of building varied little from the late sixteenth to the early nineteenth century.

might have exceeded anything More imagined for his Amaurote: it might have become the wonder of Europe. But as Samuel Pepys recorded in his *Diary*, "great differences will be, and the streets built by fits, and not entire until all differences be decided." (February 24, 1667).

Had Wren's plan for London been adopted, the whole character of English towns, the houses in them and the placing of houses in relationship to each other, might have been utterly different to-day. The idea of planning towns passed beyond the theoretical stage in eighteenth-century England; but in the seventeenth century, opportunities were lost partly because people could not understand that it was possible for individual houses to have privacy without keeping the hugger-mugger congestion of sites that had arisen in the course of the mediaeval city's growth.

In the country, planning in a grand, spacious way was already accepted. The great estates were planned. Gardens and groves, parkland, villages, were all related to the great house itself. Its outbuildings, its stables, offices and sheds, were tidily disposed. Its approaches were consciously magnificent. Tree-planting was a part of this planning; great avenues swept up to the porticos of the new country mansions; screens of trees were planted to protect the arable land from adverse winds; clumps of woodland embellished the parks; the landscape was taken under the wing of the architect, who, between the years 1660 and 1830, had an immense influence upon the appearance of the countryside and the town, and the homes, large and small, which accommodated a largely prosperous and steadily growing population. It was the golden age of English building, and during that time the nobility and gentry developed a lively and educated taste in architecture. Their taste was admired and imitated by humbler folk; but all classes of society had a respect for good materials, sensibly and imaginatively used, whether in the building of a house, a ship, a coach, or the making of a chair or a table.

The Puritan interlude had prepared the country for a change in taste. The reaction, after all the repressive laws of the Cromwellian period, was towards light-hearted extravagance. The art of living was again practised, and foreign fashions once more entered England though they were now kept under control, for patrons had better taste than in late Tudor times, and craftsmen and architects had more knowledge. Charles II's marriage to Catherine of Braganza brought in a brief mode for Portuguese decoration. The fashions, though not the habits of the court, slowly spread through the country. It was such a relief to most people to have a Merry Monarch at the head of affairs instead of a glum Dictator. Gentlemen who had found Puritan England not only intolerable but dangerous, began to fill their houses with all manner of beautiful and decorative things which they had picked up during their travels in Europe, for when the King and the Court came back, all these self-made exiles came back too. New ideas poured into the country from France, Spain, Portugal and the Far East. Everywhere gentlemen were studying architecture. They were becoming conscious of the rules of good proportion; they knew where to stop in the matter of decorating their homes, and they deserved the good architecture that men of genius like Wren could create.

Large town and country houses now acquired the dignity that good proportions can confer on buildings, but they remained friendly places. There was something genial and inviting about them; they were not exclusive in their grandeur, for Englishmen, however wealthy and fond of indulging their taste for magnificent building, never took kindly to palaces of the Continental variety. In London there were palaces, before and after the great fire of 1666; they were built mostly along the Strand, with their gardens running down to the Thames, which, despite the filth that drained into it, was a salmon river; but they were exceptional buildings, survivals from a former age. Nobody who could afford to build on a grand scale would attempt to erect anything more than a commodious town house, surrounded by as much ground as possible.

When London's new houses of neat brick, trimmed with stone-work, arose on the ruins of the old wood-and-plaster city, they were so popular that builders and landlords, to keep pace with the demand, often built over the gardens and orchards that had formerly separated blocks of dwellings, or surrounded individual houses. Many old houses, untouched by the fire, were demolished to make way for new buildings. Any thought of planning the city had faded away. Even Pepys, who was generally delighted with things as they were, deplored the way the rebuilding of London was being handled by various interests. On April 5, 1667, he mentions a conversation he had on this subject with Mr. Young, who told him "that those few churches that are to be new built are plainly not chosen with regard to the convenience of the City; they stand a great many in a cluster about Cornhill: but that all of them are either in the gift of the Lord Archbishop, or Bishop of London, or Lord Chancellor, or gift of the City. Thus all things, even to the building of churches, are done in this world!"

Although plans for making London a tidy, well-ordered city had been produced not only by Wren, but by John Evelyn and Robert Hooke, they were never carried beyond the stage of preliminary discussion: they were not even examined by Parliament or the City Corporation.[1] Meanwhile, the rebuilding of the city provided a few gifted architects with work, and the city churches designed by Wren gave London a new skyline of exquisite spires and towers, built largely of Portland stone. This material was used for some of the great new town houses, and for the window architraves and sills, the porches, the cornices and all the incidental stonework of the brick-built homes of the new and prosperous middle-class citizens, the small tradesmen and merchants and master-craftsmen, and the professional men, lawyers and civil servants, like Pepys. "Limestone from the Portland beds has won first place as a London wall surface owing to its resistance to acids and to the fact that under the combined influence of smoke and rain it turns from a cream colour into black and white. The white parts reflect the light . . ."[2]

Those town houses were luxurious; the contents of their high, well-lit rooms were increasingly varied. Furniture makers, released from Puritan prohibitions and restraints, lavished carved decoration and inlaid ornament on chairs and chests, mirror frames and day-beds, stools, tables, writing desks, and all the forms of furniture that the new and fuller life of fashionable folk demanded. Chairs were sometimes made of walnut, and canework was used for their backs and seats. The day-bed was a long seat with an adjustable head that could be lowered. Into the panelled rooms of the new houses came chests of drawers on low stands, in oak and walnut;

[1] *London: The Unique City*, by Steen Eiler Rasmussen, Chap. VI, p. 112.
[2] *Theory and Elements of Architecture*, by Robert Atkinson and Hope Bagenal, Section 8, Chap. V, p. 155.

lacquer cabinets from China, which stood on carved and gilded stands; lacquer screens; polished brass candelabra holding anything up to twelve candles; brass or silver wall sconces for candles; beds with their backs and testers covered with damask, with plumes or finials surmounting the deep damask-covered moulding of the cornice; oriental rugs and carpets and vases—all the colour and gaiety of form which the sour severity of Puritan dictatorship had discouraged. Pepys, who was not a rich man, though comfortably well off and always interested in improving his income, could afford to redecorate his dining-room "with greene serge hanging and gilt leather." At a later date he paid "near 40l. for a set of chairs and couch . . ." and mentioned his new plate which set off his cupboard "very nobly". He admired and appreciated beautiful and curious things, and among the curious objects he noted in his *Diary* was a bath, placed at the top of a house in Lincoln's Inn Fields, owned by a Mr. Povey, a gentleman who certainly practised the art of living with great thoroughness. Pepys was deeply impressed by the house. "And in a word, methinks, for his perspective in the little closet; his room floored above with woods of several colours, like but above the best cabinet-work I ever saw; his grotto and vault with his bottles of wine, and a well therein to keep them cool; his furniture of all sorts; his bath at the top of the house, good pictures, and his manner of eating and drinking; do surpass all that ever I did see of one man in all my life." Evelyn in his *Diary* backed this opinion about Mr. Povey's possessions, and in an entry on July 1, 1664, he wrote: ". . . the perspective in his court, painted by Streeter, is indeed excellent, with the vases in imitation of porphyrie, and fountains; the inlaying of his closet; above all, his pretty cellar and the ranging of his wine bottles." A bath was certainly a rare thing to find in a house. Pepys apparently had never bathed until he visited the city of Bath, and then he was rather shocked by the idea: "methinks it cannot be clean to go so many bodies together in the same water." (June 13, 1668.)

Pepys mentions an experience early in his *Diary* (September 28, 1660), which was strange at that time: he sent "for a cup of tea (a China drink) of which I never had drank before . . ." Seven years later he finds his wife making tea, "a drink which Mr. Pelling, the Potticary, tells her is good for her cold." (June 28, 1667.) Tea-drinking had not yet become a social custom, but it was to become a national habit within half a century, and to affect the form of many articles of furniture and to bring into existence hundreds of graceful things in silver and china, and when it spread to the cottage homes of England, it was to be denounced with fury by that great upholder of the "good old times", William Cobbett. Such a boisterous critic of everything un-English would certainly have approved of the sixteen-sixties and seventies if he had observed country life; though he might have scorned the fashions of the town.

New brick houses built in the country were generally rose red in colour, unless local brick had a russet or yellow hue. But bricks were usually bright red, for a century or more of weathering was needed before the brightness was toned down. The grounds of big country houses were enclosed by high brick walls, and often the walls of three or four parks or gardens would darken the lanes that led from a village, so that villagers were almost imprisoned by the landholder's desire for privacy. Such walled-in village lanes still survive in some parts of the country, and may be seen in the older parts of Petersham and Ham in Surrey and in Twickenham in Middlesex. Behind those walls the country gentry lived a full and happy life, and it was not separated from the life of the countryside, for the seventeenth-century squires rode and hunted and farmed, built new cottages, improved their property and increased the comfort of their tenants. "A country house in those days was a factory for all the best that English life could offer, making its own food and drink from seeding to brew-house and kitchen, its own fuel and candles, spinning flax and wool for clothing and upholstery, and even curing feathers to make its own mattresses and pillows."[1]

The country cottage and the small town house alike had windows glazed with rather crude, distorted glass: they had fire-places, grates, candles, cooking vessels of iron and copper, plates and mugs of pewter and earthenware, and plenty of good, simple furniture. A century and a half later, William Cobbett in his *Cottage Economy* wrote that "In household goods the *warm*, the *strong*, the *durable*, ought always to be kept in view. Oak-tables, bedsteads and stools, chairs of oak or of yew-tree, and never a bit of miserable deal board. Things of this sort ought to last several life-times. A labourer ought to inherit something besides his toil from his great-grandfather."[2] He might have been writing about the typical possessions of a farmer or cottager in the reign of Charles II. Such simple, well-made articles were handed down from father to son, and in many a cottage a chest or joint stool made by some country craftsman a century earlier, would still be in use. Oak and ash and elm were used by those gifted village craftsmen, also yew-tree, applewood and cherry-wood; and they were quite capable of making the joinery, the panelling and the staircase, the doors and window-frames, rafters, beams, trusses, joists and floors for the new house the squire happened to be building to the designs of some architect, or which he had designed himself and with the aid of local builders, carpenters and

[1] *The England of Charles II*, by Arthur Bryant, Chap. III, p. 56.
[2] Cobbett's *Cottage Economy*, paragraph 200. Quoted from the Stereotype Edition 1822.

LONDON STREET, AS RE-BUILT AFTER THE GREAT FIRE.

smiths, proposed to erect. Once more as in mediaeval times, Englishmen seemed unable to build anything ugly or stupid; and their houses, large or small, particularly in the country, reflected both the pleasure they took in the arts and the virile common sense that carried them through life.

CHAPTER XI

PROGRESS IN HOUSE DESIGN
(A.D. 1680–1700)

UNDER the last Stuart kings many foreign ideas influenced fashions in dress and furniture, but in the reign of William III Holland was the chief source of such ideas. Only one left a permanent mark on the character of every type of English house, and that particular Dutch idea was in use some time before William of Orange had replaced James II, for it was from Holland that the sash-window was first introduced. The word "sash" comes from the Dutch *sas*, meaning sluice, and the French *chassis*, meaning frame.[1] Such windows were generally in the form of a double square, consisting of the upper and the lower sash, which slid up and down and had balance weights which allowed either sash to remain in any position. The sashes were usually divided vertically by two glazing bars and horizontally by one, so that each sash had six rectangular panes of glass. In large windows the sashes would be divided by three vertical and two horizontal glazing bars, which doubled the number of panes, giving twelve to each sash and twenty-four to the whole window. But the rectangular window was still generally based on the proportion of the double square, though there were exceptions to this rule. When sash windows were fitted to the entrance front of Raynham Hall, Norfolk, the lower sashes were square with six panes, the upper sashes rectangular with nine panes. The sashes that replaced the original windows of Inigo Jones's Banqueting Hall in Whitehall in 1685 had sixteen panes in each, thirty-two panes to a window, formed by three vertical and two horizontal glazing bars to each sash. Wren used this type of thirty-two pane window to light the first floor of Hampton Court Palace, on the South and East sides. The glazing bars were of wood, and the glass was fixed with putty.

The quality of the glass used was much improved, for after the Revocation of the Edict of Nantes, many highly skilled Huguenot glassmakers settled in England. An advertisement in the *London Gazette*, June 4, 1691, not only shows the extent to which sash windows were in general use, but suggests that English glassmakers had high confidence in their products. "There is now made at the Bear-garden Glass-House on the Bank-side Crown Window Glass, much exceeding French Glass in all its Qualifications, which may be

---

[1] *Theory and Elements of Architecture*, by Robert Atkinson and Hope Bagenal, Chap. IX, Section 6, p. 333.

SEVENTEENTH- AND EARLY EIGHTEENTH-CENTURY WINDOWS

Left: This type of window, divided centrally by a stone mullion, with a stone transome dividing the upper part horizontally, was in use in large houses until the late seventeenth century. *Centre:* The early double sash windows were based on the proportion of a double square, each sash divided vertically by three glazing bars and horizontally by two, forming twelve panes. *Right:* Early in the eighteenth century the double sash window had larger panes and fewer glazing bars. The proportion of the double square was generally retained throughout the Georgian period.

squared into all sizes of Sashes for windows and other uses. . . "[1] Convenient, well-proportioned windows were available, and although casements and mullioned windows were still used, the sash window had come to stay, and it became identified with English domestic building. In 1697 a window tax was levied on houses with more than six windows and worth over £5 per annum. This tax checked the use of windows, and it remained until 1851, a dark and cramping influence on house design.

By the end of the seventeenth century, small houses had been greatly improved in design, and a compact, space-saving device had at last solved the problem of the staircase. In houses with two or more storeys the stairs had risen from the entrance hall, ascending to a gallery or landing that overlooked the hall, an arrangement that occupied considerable space and gave great dignity to the stairway, but in a small house it was an inconvenient waste of space. To save this space the dog-legged stair was invented. This was a

[1] Quoted by Raymond McGrath and A. C. Frost in *Glass in Architecture and Decoration*, Section II, p. 97.

flight of stairs with a half-landing between the floors—the commonest type in use to-day. When first introduced it was known as "a pair of stairs".

Small town houses were often built in terraces; so the courtyard vanished, and the garden shrank in size. Some of the terraces built in London were elegant pieces of architecture, and they gave new unity to streets; six or more houses could be treated as one architectural composition, like the front of one great mansion. Some terraces were built by landlords as a speculation, for people were crowding into London and other cities and towns, and there was a growing demand for accommodation. Everywhere towns were being enlarged or rebuilt, and some of them like London had been damaged by fire. "Northampton, having ben lately burnt and re-edified, is now become a town that for the beauty of the buildings, especialy the church and town-house, may compare with the neatest in Italy itself," wrote Evelyn in his *Diary*, July 23, 1688. Some towns produced a local architect of genius, like Henry Bell of King's Lynn. That town on the Wash was prosperous, and its prosperity was recorded in brick and stone not only by the fine houses of the merchants, but by its Custom House and the great tavern in the market place, the Duke's Head, both designed by Bell.[1]

The building of houses in terraces encouraged a tendency to make the street frontage showy, and to leave the backs untidy. Landlords were sometimes greedy, and the amount of space allowed for gardens behind terrace houses of the poorer type was reduced to a cramped strip of ground. Noblemen who had given up big, old-fashioned houses in London, let them out in floors and groups of rooms or single rooms, to all kinds and conditions of people; they gradually became squalid tenements; dirt, misery and over-crowding were found in what had once been palaces, and Queen Elizabeth's humanitarian decree that only one family should inhabit a dwelling was utterly forgotten: it had seldom been obeyed. A century later Dr. Samuel Johnson was to remind his fellow-Londoners that "In London . . . a man's own house is truly his *castle*, in which he can be in perfect safety from intrusion. . . ." But he was thinking only of householders, not of the inhabitants of the tenements and lodging houses, who shared a common stairway with perhaps a dozen families in a narrow-fronted, three-storied house in some terrace, built in the late seventeenth century, and far gone in decay at the time the Doctor was writing.

The brick walls that separated the houses in a terrace also accommodated the flues from the fire-places, and chimney stacks rose above

---

[1] Two-and-a-half centuries later, Lynn produced another architect, famous for his revival of the simple traditions of English domestic building. He was the late Sir Guy Dawber, R.A., F.S.A., President of the Royal Institute of British Architects in 1928.

SUSSEX HOMESTEAD

An example of the brick built house of the late seventeenth and eighteenth centuries.

the level of the roof ridge. There was a great increase in the number of fire-places, nearly every room had one except the attics under the roof. In the basement, which was the lowest storey of the building and partly or wholly below ground level, the kitchen fire-place would still retain some of its ancient magnitude, brick ovens forming hobs, with a wrought iron grate and a cast-iron fireback. The basements of terrace houses were often dark and gloomy places, sometimes approached from the street by a separate stairway, descending from the pavement to the area. In the larger town houses the servants worked and lived in the basement, and slept in the attics. In the smaller houses, only those who could afford nothing better lived in the basement rooms.

The countryman was still better off in his cottage than the townsman in his lodgings. There were, as yet, no rural slums. The servant in the country house enjoyed healthier conditions than the town mansion provided. The life and character of a great country house in the last years of the century is described by Evelyn. "The house, or rather palace, at Althorp, is a noble uniform pile in form of a half H, built of brick and freestone, ballustred and *a la moderne*; the hall is well, the staircase excellent; the roomes of state, gallerys, offices and furniture, such as may become a greate Prince. It is situate in the midst of a garden, exquisitely planted and kept, and all this in a parke wall'd in with hewn stone, planted with rows and walkes of trees, canals and fish ponds, and stor'd with game. And what is above all this, govern'd by a lady, who without any shew

STONE-BUILT COTTAGES ON THE DIGE, ST. IVES
Each house has its individual character, although the same
building methods and materials are used.

of sollicitude, keepes every thing in such admirable order, both
within and without, from the garret to the cellar, that I do not
believe there is any in this nation, or in any other, that exceedes her
in such exact order, without ostentation, but substantially greate
and noble. The meanest servant is lodg'd so neat and cleanly;
the service at the several tables, the good order and decency—in a
word, the intire oeconomy, is perfectly becoming a wise and noble
person." (July 18, 1688.)

Those country houses, great and small, were chosen and designed by men of taste, and in some smooth, well-turned verses, a gentleman of the period described the sort of home that would satisfy his standards of life.

> "Near some fair Town I'd have a private Seat
> Built uniform; not little, nor too great;
> Better if on a rising ground it stood;
> On this side fields, on that a neighb'ring wood.
> It should, within, no other Things contain
> But what were Useful, Necessary, Plain:
> Methinks 'tis nauseous, and I'd ne'er endure
> The needless Pomp of gaudy furniture."

The lines written in 1699, occur in *The Choice or Wish: A Poem written by a Person of Quality*. The poet was John Pomfret, a country clergyman, rector of Maulden in Bedfordshire.

Few country gentlemen felt a desire for "the needless pomp of gaudy furniture", but in their homes, and in the homes of merchants and professional men in the towns, furniture had increased in variety and convenience. Walnut tables and cabinets, chests of drawers and chests mounted on stands with turned or twisted legs, long-case clocks, chairs with upholstered seats and backs, were arrayed in those pleasant rooms with their well-proportioned sash windows, and their oak panelled walls. Of all the articles that improved the furnishing of the late seventeenth century house, clocks were the most remarkable. The brass lantern clock perched high on its bracket with its weights and swinging pendulum had developed into a handsome article, with the works enclosed in a hooded frame, and the weights and pendulum accommodated in a long case of oak or walnut. These long-case or "grandfather" clocks were made in many parts of the country, for English craftsmen were everywhere demonstrating their mechanical genius. Thomas Tompion, the greatest of English clockmakers, was the eldest son of a blacksmith, and was born at Northill, Bedfordshire, in 1639. Early in the eighteenth century he became Master of the Clockmakers' Company, and when he died in 1713, was buried in Westminster Abbey. Daniel Quare, Joseph Knibb, Christopher Gould and Cornelius Herbert were all London clockmakers; but every small town, and many villages, had clockmakers, men who applied the horological discoveries of such scientists as Dr. Robert Hooke and the Reverend Edward Barlow.[1]

In the interior decoration of rooms, the panelling, or wainscotting as it was called, derived its proportions from those laid down for the Roman orders of architecture: the dado corresponding to the plinth, the space between the dado and the frieze approximating to the height of the column, and the frieze and cornice representing

---

[1] *Masterpieces of English Furniture and Clocks*, by R. W. Symonds, Chap. VI, p. 95.

BRACKET CLOCK, 1660

The latter part of the seventeenth century witnessed the
development of English clock-making. The early clocks stood
high on the wall, on brackets to allow room for the weights
and pendulum.

the entablature. Thus inside and out, the English home was governed by a system of design that architects used with imagination.
Into that system the sash window and the chimney breast with its
fire-place and mantel-piece fitted admirably, and the result was a
national architecture "built uniform", unpretentious and homely
in the best sense of that word. Even when the greatest of English
architects rebuilt a palace for King William, the national gift for
creating homes gave more than mere magnificence to the design.
Sir Christopher Wren's additions to Hampton Court Palace have
the same intimate air of comfort that any English house of the time
possessed.

Wherever men built in the countryside, they thought beyond
their own lifetimes. Every new cottage or farmhouse was well
placed: the landlord would not allow new buildings to mar a view.

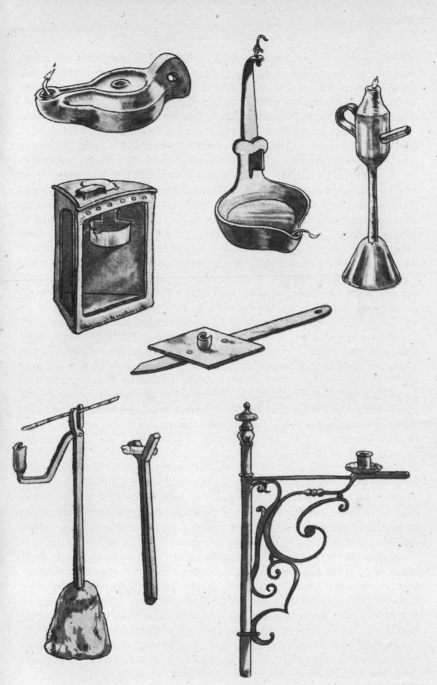

LAMPS AND CANDLESTICKS

A variety of methods for providing sockets for candles, or reservoirs of oil for wicks.

These men had a sensitive regard for beauty. They planted trees, laid out gardens, and rearranged the landscape to suit their critical fancy. The chestnut avenue at Bushey Park, and hundreds of other avenues and groves of trees that grow more slowly than chestnut, were planted with patient vision: the improvement of an estate demanded this unselfishness, and a landowner thought of his sons and his grandsons. Also, he knew that timber was a crop, which in due time could be reaped for the benefit of some future generation of his family. In the last decades of the century the Norway Maple and the Cedar of Lebanon had been introduced, and cedars with their dark green shelving foliage were in great favour as ornamental trees. Planting and building in the country might be inspired by a sense of responsibility to future generations, but in the towns, and particularly in London, that sense was often lacking. Here and there some terrace or street would be planned and planted, but these were piecemeal efforts, small in scale though agreeable enough in appearance. None the less, London still had trees and gardens, with an occasional orchard, or some solitary fruit tree to mark the site of an orchard that had been sacrificed to the needs of new building.

During the course of the century several squares had been laid out, and about these open spaces fashionable residences were built. Leicester Square had been made in front of Leicester House as early as 1635, Bloomsbury Square in 1665 and Red Lion Square, north of Lincoln's Inn Fields, in 1684. The western growth of London was rapid after the Great Fire. Soho Square was laid out in 1681, St. James's Square in 1684, Grosvenor Square in 1695 and Berkeley Square in 1698. Of these, St. James's Square was the best example of well planned development, and it became and remained a fashionable quarter. Even so it failed to satisfy some critics. Half a century later the anonymous writer of *A Critical Review of the Public Buildings, Statues and Ornaments, in, and about, London and Westminster*,[1] said that "*St. James's Square* has an appearance of grandeur superior to any other plan in town, and yet there is not any one elegant houfe in it; and the fide next Pall-Mall is fcandaloufly rude and irregular. . ."

Architects in the golden age of building seldom forgot that their work would be appraised by gentlemen who had studied architecture, and who knew what they were talking about when they criticised the design of a building. The patrons of architecture and the critics and writers set a high standard, and it was a standard based on knowledge, not on ignorant whims and prejudices. When the seventeenth century began, English taste in house building had been muddled by foreign ideas; at the close of the century a national domestic architecture had been created and established.

---

[1] Printed by C. Ackers in St. John's Street, for J. Wilford behind the chapter house in St. Paul's Churchyard, and J. Clarke at the Golden Ball in Duck Lane, 1734.

LATE SEVENTEENTH CENTURY HOUSE IN A SMALL COUNTRY TOWN.

CHAPTER XII

QUEEN ANNE AND EARLY GEORGIAN HOMES

(A.D. 1700–1750)

QUEEN ANNE gave her name to a period that is always regarded as typically English, both for the deep comfort of the houses built at that time, and for the simple and graceful lines of the furniture they contained. Actually, it was a period in which a good many foreign ideas acquired English forms. In the previous reign, Dutch curves had appeared in furniture; Dutch officials had appeared at court, Dutch officers in the Army and Navy, and friends of the Dutch king were everywhere; so very naturally Dutch fashions invaded many branches of English life. But English furniture-makers refined the rather swollen and heavy shapes that were favoured by Dutch taste in furniture, and in the opening years of the eighteenth century, large town and country houses had some of the most beautiful furniture that has ever been made. Strong, simple, yet elegant in form, the furniture of the Queen Anne period has never been surpassed, either for comfort or beauty. It has sometimes been claimed that the perfect solution for the chair as a piece of design, using wood as a material, was reached in those years. The legs of chairs were now separated, they were not tied together by stretchers; perhaps stretchers were no longer necessary, as floors were clean and carpeted, and there was no need to tuck your feet up on a rail under the chair, to avoid contact with dirty rushes.

Chairs whose legs had outward curving knees, cabriole legs as they were called, appeared in the dining-rooms and drawing-rooms and boudoirs of well-furnished houses. Chair-backs were set at a slight angle, and curved to provide greater comfort for those who sat in them.

Walnut was now the wood chiefly used for furniture-making, and on the fronts of drawers and cupboards, clock cases and bureaux, beautiful veneers of this wood were inlaid with elaborate and intricate floral patterns. The woods used for inlay or marqueterie included holly, box, yew, sycamore, apple, pear, bog oak and beech. The nature of inlay and marqueterie has been aptly defined by H. P. Shapland: "Strictly speaking inlaid work should be regarded as the technique which consists of forming slight sinkings of an eighth or quarter of an inch deep in the solid wood, and then filling the hollows so made with woods of a different colour, cut to fit them. Marqueterie is a later development and is closely bound up with veneering. In marqueterie the ornament is first cut into a thin sheet of wood or veneer and subsequently the veneer and ornament, as one sheet, are applied to the surface of the wood."[1]

Veneering was a highly skilled craft; it was not a dodge for covering up inferior wood with a thin layer of a more expensive material.

Modern comfort in furnishing really had its origin in the early years of the eighteenth century. Although upholstered furniture had appeared in the last few years of the previous century, it was scarce and confined to the wealthiest homes; but with the opening years of Queen Anne's reign, upholstered furniture came into general use. High-backed, easy chairs with wings and wide, rolled arms, stuffed seats and sides and backs, provided a framework for the be-wigged and marvellously clothed gentlemen who sat bolt upright, their artificial curls cascading over their shoulders. Their lace and jewellery, their buckled shoes and silk stockings, their coats of gorgeous colour, and their gold and silver laced waistcoats, were elegantly set off by the damask or needlework that covered those tall chairs.

Every room in the town house of the period was thronged with convenient and decorative articles of furniture. Mirrors in walnut frames, edged with gilded ornament, threw back reflections from every wall: curtains of rich fabrics could be drawn across the windows, and well-proportioned windows gave a good and cheerful light to every room. Vertical windows which are carried up fairly close to the ceiling provide by far the best lighting for a room, because it is through the upper panes of a window that most of the daylight enters. Most houses bore the marks of the light tax, and blind windows, bricked up and painted outside in black and white to match those that really admitted light, were to be found in houses, large and small, in town and country.

In the country, farm labourers and country folk were still housed in dwellings built by traditional methods, and of the same materials as those used by their immediate forebears. Their furniture was of the simplest and plainest kind. Here and there on the great estates, in the villages and small towns, were little brick-built houses and cottages, inhabited by gardeners, gamekeepers, small shopkeepers and well-to-do artisans, and these were furnished with an increasing variety of country-made objects.

While the fashionable furniture-makers of the town might produce elegant chairs, curved to accommodate with dignity and comfort the fashionable figures of elaborately dressed ladies and gentlemen, in the country chair-makers had worked out a design

[1] *Practical Decoration of Furniture*, by H. P. Shapland, Vol. I, "Inlay or Marqueterie", p. 17.

TIMBER HOUSES IN KENT

From the late eighteenth to the early nineteenth centuries, timber was used, in the form of weatherboarding, for the exterior of houses in some parts of Kent, Surrey, Sussex, Essex and Middlesex. The chimney stacks were of brick.

that has for over two centuries become deeply associated with English country furnishing. The stick-back, or Windsor chair, was invented in the early years of the eighteenth century. The wood seat is shaped, and its pattern was originally made from a clay model. The depressions formed by anybody sitting on a slab of damp clay gave the chair-maker the proper shape for a comfortable seat. This seat is often of elm; the legs, and spindles of the back are usually of beech; the bow frame of the back and the arms are of yew. Beech is turned easily, yew is curved easily, elm is shaped easily. The English craftsman has always selected the most appropriate materials.

These chairs, in the course of the eighteenth century, became common; they would be found in every farm-house and inn and in many cottages. Sometimes they would follow town fashions; stick-back chairs with cabriole legs were made, and a central splat with a decorative device would be used in the back. But although chairs became more common in furnishing the cottage and farm-house, the possessions of the countryman were, by modern standards, rather scanty, though by old Cobbett's sturdy standards they were ample. The country cottage may have been bare, but the household goods were warm, strong and durable.

Although a few small brick houses had been built, traditional and local materials and building habits still determined the appearance and character of most cottages. In some parts of the country, in the districts around Brandon in Norfolk and in parts of Sussex, for example, flints were embedded in cement and made excellent walls. Countrymen still lived in wooden-framed houses with plaster walls and thatched roofs. The plaster-work was finished off with decorative patterns which varied from district to district, each district having its characteristic features, so that the traveller who was familiar with them, could tell by glancing at a wall, which county he was in. In Essex and Kent and some districts of Middlesex, Surrey and Sussex, houses were faced with wooden boards, overlapping each other like courses of tiles. Many of them still survive. These houses with clap-boards or weather-boards, as they are called, were easy to build. They consisted of a brick chimney stack, a tiled roof, wooden framing, painted wooden walls outside and plastered walls inside. During the eighteenth century, considerable numbers of such houses were built all over the south country. Sometimes the walls of the ground floor would be of brick, with weather-boarding on the upper storey; sometimes the upper storey would have tiles hung on wooden battens, and this tiled finish was frequently used in Sussex.

In the new small houses and cottages, the sash window was gradually introduced. The small country house in general appearance began to reflect the country gentleman's taste in architecture. The prosperity of the countryside, and the continual improvement of large and small estates, was due to the vital interest most landowners took in country life. Their lives were of the pattern described in the opening verses of Pope's *Ode to Solitude*.

"Happy the man, whose wish and care
A few paternal acres bound,
Content to breathe his native air
In his own ground.

"Whose herds with milk, whose fields with bread,
Whose flocks supply him with attire,
Whose trees in summer yield him shade,
In winter fire."

The continental landowner, particularly in France, often regarded his estate merely as a source of money, where rents were collected by efficient managers: abroad, tenants and landlords were separated by social custom, in England they were both part of a lively and vigorous community. The squire's house was a well-found, well-built place, and although a nobleman might occasionally make a costly experiment in magnificence, neither the nobility nor the gentry cared much for palaces. The countryfolk had a way of calling any exhibition of architectural extravagance a "folly". One English architect of the early eighteenth century, Sir John Vanbrugh, designed great country houses, which were palaces on the continental scale; they never found much favour with Englishmen. Vanbrugh was made Comptroller of the Royal Works under Sir Christopher Wren in 1702; he had been a soldier, and a successful writer of plays; he began his career as an architect when he was over forty. He built Blenheim Palace for the Duke of Marlborough; it has been described as "the most monumental mansion in England."[1]

Vanbrugh, in a letter, once said he was making some alterations to a house "both for state, beauty and convenience."[2] As an architect he specialised in stateliness: few Englishmen desired to be stately. As works of architecture, his great houses are superb. Castle Howard, in Yorkshire, Seaton Delaval in Northumberland, and Blenheim certainly have "state" and "beauty"; but Pope's verses on Blenheim show how in general his countrymen reacted to such grandeur.

> "See, sir, here's the grand approach;
> This way is for his grace's coach:
> There lies the bridge, and here's the clock,
> Observe the lion and the cock,
> The spacious court, the colonnade,
> And mark how wide the hall is made!
> The chimneys are so well design'd,
> They never smoke in any wind.
> This gallery's contrived for walking,
> The windows to retire and talk in;
> The council chamber for debate,
> And all the rest are rooms of state.
> Thanks, sir, cried I, 'tis very fine,
> But where d'ye sleep, or where d'ye dine?
> I find, by all you have been telling,
> That 'tis a house, but not a dwelling."

James Branston, in *The Man of Taste*, also criticised the scale of Vanbrugh's work.

> "Substantial walls and heavy roofs I like,
> 'Tis Vanbrugh's structures that my fancy strike;
> Such noble ruins every pile would make,
> I wish they'd tumble for the prospect's sake."

[1] *A History of Architecture on the Comparative Method*, by Sir Banister Fletcher. English Renaissance section, p. 734. (Eighth edition.)
[2] Quoted by Christian Barman in his short study, *Sir John Vanbrugh*. ("Masters of Architecture" series), p. 24.

Abel Evans suggested this epitaph for the architect:

"Under this stone, reader, survey
Dead Sir John Vanbrugh's house of clay.
Lie heavy on him, earth! for he
Laid many heavy loads on thee."

The Earl of Burlington improved the architectural taste of his contemporaries by publishing the designs of Inigo Jones and Palladio's drawings of the "Antiquities of Rome". Pope expressed some fears that such educational work would be misunderstood, and that their chief effect would be to "Fill half the land with imitating fools . . ."

But the use of the Roman orders of architecture had long been advanced from the stage of unintelligent copying. The publication of Palladio's drawings certainly led to a more widespread use c classical designs, and the term Palladian became associated with the elegant houses of the early Georgian period. It was an age of architectural understanding. Gentlemen could discuss the details of any design with their architects, for their interests and their education equipped them with the knowledge and ability to do so with intelligence. The country builders could buy books on architecture, which gave good directions for building in accordance with the rules of the Roman orders, and as those rules and standards of design were everywhere accepted, and as they were combined with the use of such well-proportioned units as the double sash window, a new house, large or small, was never an eyesore.

In the towns brick had come into common use. For large or small houses it was the most convenient material; only when local stone was plentiful or when some grand effect was desired was stone used in cities. Bath, which was replanned and rebuilt in stone during the first part of the eighteenth century, was one of the finest examples of town planning in England. It was the work of two architects, both named John Wood, a father and son, and to their genius Bath owes its orderly beauty. As a city it was made tidy and its streets were designed not piecemeal, but as a whole: each house had its place; noble terraces and arcades flowed along its spacious thoroughfares; it was adorned by such superb pieces of architectural composition as the Royal Crescent and the Circus: not since the days of Roman Britain had a city been so well planned, and the rebuilding of Bath emphasised how much London had lost by rejecting a new street plan after the Great Fire.

London was still growing, it was spreading into the surrounding fields, transforming villages into suburbs, and it was being developed by great landlords and speculative builders. West and north the fields and market gardens gave place to houses; and the building development was sometimes skilfully planned, as the writer of the

MARKET SQUARE IN SMALL COUNTRY TOWN, EARLY EIGHTEENTH CENTURY.

Critical Review, quoted earlier, was prepared to admit. In describing Queen's Square and Southampton Row, he shows how such schemes were planned in relation to the prospect of the open countryside, although the thought of those who planned them did not reach far enough ahead to anticipate the unceasing growth that would in time destroy the prospect and enclose them with other buildings.

"Queens-Square," he wrote, "is an area of a peculiar kind, being left open on one fide, for the fake of the beautiful landfcape, which is form'd by the hills of Highgate and Hampftead, together with the adjacent fields; a delicacy which deferves fome approbation, both as 'tis an advantage to the inhabitants, and a beauty even with regard to the square itfelf.

"Southampton-Row is a range of buildings, which feems to have been built only for the fake of the profpect before it, and for fuch who prefer no conveniency to that, no fituation can be more happy; but for my own part, I fhould be uneafy in refiding there, for want of fhelter from the wind in winter, and the fun in fummer."[1]

The new brick houses were simple and well-proportioned. The stone facings and ornaments; the entrance doors, flanked by columns which supported the roof of the porch, or protected by a hood carried on carved brackets if there was not enough space for a porch; the tall windows; the general air of bright neatness without and the suggestion of comfort within, made these houses the most remarkably pleasant places to inhabit. The mark of refined taste served by good workmanship was visible everywhere. The area railings were beautiful examples of wrought ironwork; the two inverted cones by the entrance door, which served to extinguish the link bearers' torches, were part of a graceful design which helped to enliven the exterior of the house. During this century of elegant building the use of such wrought iron detail greatly increased. Steps ascending to the front door were protected by ironwork rails that followed the swelling curves of the staircase balustrade inside, curves which were dictated by the wide spreading hoops worn by the women who lived in the house.

A typical town house of the early eighteenth century is described in an advertisement published in 1710. It reads thus: "To be Let, A New, Brick House, Built after the Newest Fashion, the Rooms wainscotted and Painted, Lofty Stories, Marble Foot paces to the Chimneys, Sash Windows, glaised with fine Crown Glass, large half Pace Stairs, that 2 People may go up a Breast, in a new pleasant Court planted with Vines, Jesamin, and other Greens, next Door to the Crown near Saracen's Head Inn in Carter Lane, near St. Paul's Church Yard, London."[2]

For the well-to-do citizen, spacious houses were available, but

---

[1] 1734. See Chap. XI, p. 106.
[2] Quoted in *Social Life in the Reign of Queen Anne*, by John Ashton.

spaciousness was still a novelty and was mentioned as an attraction in advertisements for houses to let. The newly-introduced dog-legged stairs were wide enough for two people to go up abreast. Another house advertisement, of 1712, after describing the ample shop and warehouse accommodation of the lower storeys, continues thus: "There is above Stairs 4 Rooms on a Floor, almost all Wainscotted, and a large Staircase all Wainscotted. All the Flat is covered with a very thick Lead, with Rails and Bannisters round the Lead and a large Cupolo on the Top. Inquire of Mr. Richard Wright, at the Perriwig in Bread Street."[1]

The interior of the town house was much richer and more elaborate than the outside. Almost all the rooms were panelled, the woods chiefly used being oak, cedar and occasionally walnut, or, in the more modest house, painted deal. Wallpapers were also coming into use. At the beginning of the century they were mostly of English make and printed to imitate tapestry, damask or embroidery. Advertisements for these wallpapers appeared in the News Sheets; one of these published in *The Postman*, December 10–12, 1702, refers to "imitation of Marbles and other Coloured Wainscots; others in yard wide, Emboss'd work, and a curious sort of Flock work. . . . ."

Towards the middle of the century fine hand-painted Chinese wallpapers were often imported and were used to cover the walls of rooms entirely, even the doors. Such papers were generally patterned with great sprays of peonies and bamboo and other flowering plants; brilliantly coloured and fantastic birds perched on the branches, and sometimes Chinese figures were also introduced, but as a rule the patterns were purely floral.

The wood panelling, or wainscotting, was sometimes left in its natural colour and wax polished, sometimes stained and polished and often, where the wood was not of a fine quality or figure, painted. Later in the century the paint was usually in white or some pale colour, but up to about 1730 it was generally of a dark hue such as brown or deep green, though occasionally bright colour was used. Sometimes gilding flashed on the carved enrichment of mouldings. Rooms in the first half of the century were inclined to be sombre; the heavy mouldings of the wall panelling, mantel-pieces and doors, the long thick curtains which draped the windows, all contributed to this effect. The window curtains were generally made of damask, brocade, or Spitalfields silk velvet, and were rich rather than brilliant in colouring. The increasing use of mirrors helped to lighten these darkly rich rooms. The fashion for displaying in cabinets or open cupboards or niches collections of Oriental porcelain and the occasional use of pieces of furniture in brightly coloured Chinese lacquer also relieved the darkness of the background.

[1] Quoted in *Social Life in the Reign of Queen Anne*, by John Ashton.

EARLY EIGHTEENTH-CENTURY GRANDFATHER CLOCK

Long-case clocks were introduced into many homes; not only would they be
found in large town and country houses but in farmhouses, where simple
copies of fashionable designs, made by local clock-makers, were used.

The furniture of the early Georgian period was richly ornamented. The simplicity that had distinguished Queen Anne furniture was lost, and the legs of chairs and tables were heavily carved and often gilded. The knees of cabriole legs would be carved with acanthus leaf or shell devices; the feet would end in a bird's claw, grasping a ball, or in some beast's paw or even a shaggy hoof. The influence of the architect was extending, and elaborate furniture was designed by men like William Kent. Such furniture was monumental in effect; the architect seemed to regard the design of a bookcase or a bureau or a side table as a small scale building problem; and the results were little architectural compositions within a room. Kent, whose patron was the Earl of Burlington, was prepared to accept responsibility for the design of anything; he built great houses like Holkham Hall, altered and decorated Kensington Palace, designed the Horse Guards, laid out gardens, devised the most impressive decoration for rooms, and loaded chimney-pieces, tables, bookcases and other articles of furniture with masses of carved and gilded ornament. Before the century was out, the architect had become the universal designer, and was prepared and able to design anything, from a great mansion to a cottage, and to be responsible moreover for the design of everything within a house.

The first effect of the increasing influence of the architect, was the introduction of Roman ornament on furniture. The enriched mouldings on such architectural features as cornices, the egg-and-dart and the bead-and-reel running ornaments, were used. Articles such as bookcases and double chests, tallboys as they were called, had moulded cornices; mirror frames were crowned by broken pediments; the mirror-fronted doors of bureau-bookcases were framed by fluted pilasters, supporting an entablature, and making the upper part look like the entrance doorway to a house. But this furniture was never ill-proportioned or badly made. It was more varied in shape and style than hitherto, and several pieces of furniture which are commonplace to-day made their first appearance in Early Georgian times. Among these were the corner cupboard, the bureau, the bureau-bookcase and the double chest of drawers. The first corner cupboards were generally tall pieces of furniture with open shelves in the upper part, and a cupboard below. Hanging corner cupboards, usually with closed doors, were used later in the century.

Settees had upholstered seats and wooden backs, shaped like chair backs. Upholstery was always used for the seats of occasional or dining-room chairs. All chair seats were broad, and arms curved outwards to accommodate the wide-skirted coats men wore, and the billowing paniers and hoops of women's dresses.

For the first thirty years of the century, walnut was the most popular wood, but after that it was rapidly supplanted by mahogany, which by 1750 was used almost exclusively for cabinet making.

A material called gesso, made of whitening and size and forming a coating on wood, was used on mirror frames, tables and chairs. It could be readily carved, and it was painted or gilded.

There were now many kinds of chairs and a variety of tables—side tables, card tables, tripod tables and the tea tables demanded by the growing fashion for what was still regarded as a novel and exotic drink. The most important and decorative single piece of furniture was the bed. This was nearly always a four-poster, even in the small house, and was enormous by modern standards, for a bed seven feet wide by eight feet long was not at all unusual. The back was still filled by a panel of wood, the tester being of wood and sometimes of stretched fabric. The tester and mattress valances were made of some rich stuff to match the bed and window curtains. The valance was cut into fanciful shapes, bound with braid and trimmed with a fringe of silk thread. Heavy cords and tassels were used to fasten back the curtains. The materials used for hangings were of the richest and heaviest kind, though lighter silks came into fashion about the middle of the century.

The richly ornamented furniture of the fashionable town house was illuminated by innumerable candles at night, hanging from the moulded and painted ceiling in candelabra with one, two or three tiers of sockets. These elaborate fittings were made of brass, silver or carved wood and gesso, painted and gilded. From brackets on the wall, other candles shed a soft and gentle light, and all these tiny flames increased the temperature of rooms. They needed constant attention, and in a large room during a party a servant had to be on duty to snuff the candles. Single candlesticks were made of brass, iron and pewter, and in the country those materials were generally used. The period was remarkable for the fine work of silversmiths, and spoons, forks, salt-cellars, sugar castors, cream jugs and tea-trays were beautifully wrought and embellished, the ornamentation being based on the forms used in architecture. In 1742 a new process of coating copper with silver was accidentally discovered by a metal worker named Thomas Bolsover. This process was developed in Sheffield, and many articles were made with this thin veneer of silver, and the combination of metals was known as Sheffield Plate.

In all branches of metal work, experiments in design were made, and many of these came under the direction of architects. Basket-grates of wrought iron, fire-backs and fire-place linings, tongs and shovels, were often designed to match. The chimney-piece was the most important decorative feature in a room. The fire-place was a national institution, and its furnishing was increasingly elaborate and efficient. The hearths or "foot paces" were of marble.

In the kitchen the open fire was still in use, although in private houses baking ovens were to be found. The bulk of the cooking was done on great spits or in pots swung over the fire, though smaller pieces of meat were sometimes cooked in a type of Dutch oven in front of the open fire.

In the new houses in some quarters of London, water from the Thames was available. An elaborate system of wheels and pumping engines raised the water, which flowed to the house through small bore wooden pipes. Apart from this pumped water, pumps and wells provided a doubtful supply to groups of houses, and drinking water from the New River was hawked about the streets by water carriers, bearing a couple of wooden barrels from shoulder yokes.

There were no baths in private houses, and although clothes were frequently washed, few people washed with any thoroughness. There were some bathing establishments, and an advertisement in *The Postman*, November 18, 1701, reads as follows: "This is to give notice, that at the Hummums, in Covent Garden, persons may sweat in the cleanest and be cupped after the newest manner. There is likewise good lodgings for any persons who choose to lodge there all night."

There were few house drains; rain water gushed from the gutters into the roadway, and flowed down the kennel. Sanitation had improved; by night, carts collected the slop pails which had formerly been emptied into the street, and took their contents to pits in the fields outside the city. The cities of eighteenth century England were still vastly inferior to those of the prosperous Roman province of Britain in matters of drainage, sewage disposal and water supply. Only in architecture and furnishing had the standards of Roman civilisation been surpassed, and never before had so many capable and talented architects been given so many opportunities. Their work, and the work of builders up and down the country, was marked by a respect for fitness in the choice of materials, and a respect for privacy in the making of plans. Pope managed to express in a couplet the thought that always guided those who made English homes the envy of the world:

"'Tis use alone that sanctifies expense,
And splendour borrows all her rays from sense."

CHAPTER XIII

LATE EIGHTEENTH-CENTURY HOUSES
(A.D. 1750–1800)

IN the month of August, 1784, a famous French nobleman wrote a letter describing his arrival in England and his journey to London. He was the Comte de Mirabeau, and his impressions of the English countryside and English houses are of special interest, for the French were the leaders of European fashion and taste in the eighteenth century, and Mirabeau had an observant and lively mind. "From Lewes," he wrote, "we traversed the finest country in Europe, for variety and verdure, for beauty and richness, for rural neatness and elegance. It was a feast for the sight, a charm for the mind, which it is impossible to exaggerate.

"The approaches to London are through a country for which Holland affords no parallel (I should compare to it some of the vallies of Switzerland), for, and this remarkable observation seizes immediately an experienced mind, this sovereign people are, above all, farmers in the bosom of their island; and that is what has so long saved it from its own convulsions. I felt my mind deeply and strongly interested as I travelled through this well cultivated and prosperous country, and I said to myself, whence this new emotion. Their castles, compared to ours, are but pigeon houses. Several cantons in France, even in the poorest provinces, and all Normandy, which I have just visited, are finer by nature than these fields. Here we find in this place, and that place, but every where in our country, fine edifices, proud buildings, great public works, the traces of the most wonderful works of man; and yet this contents me more than those things astonish me. It is that nature is here ameliorated and not forced . . . that the high state of cultivation here announces the respect for property; that this care and universal neatness is a living system of well being; that all this rural wealth is in nature, by nature, according to nature, and does not disclose that extreme inequality of fortune, source of so many evils, like the sumptuous edifice surrounded by cottages; it is that here every thing informs me that the people are something; that every man has the development and free exercise of his faculties, and that thus I am in a new order of things."[1]

This "rural neatness and elegance" was not peculiar to the prosperous counties of Sussex and Surrey through which Mirabeau

---

[1] An extract from Mirabeau's letter was included in *La Decade Philosophique Literaire et Politique*, and the translation from which the quotation is made appeared in *The European Magazine*, November 1798.

travelled to London: everywhere the English countryside had benefited by the planning of far-sighted landowners who, a hundred years earlier, had laid out parks and planted trees for their great-grandchildren. It was a secure and orderly world, and foreign wars and changes of fashion made little difference to country life and country ways. While trees long planted grew to maturity, and arable land, cultivated by improved methods, yielded richer harvests, the growing towns of the Midlands and the North were year by year, invading the country. To those swollen towns increasing numbers of countrymen were attracted, year after year, for the industrial revolution was beginning, although nobody at the time suspected that any change was taking place. It was not thought of as a revolution at all, although it ultimately changed the face of the land, ruined most of the towns, and led to the building of thousands of hideous and insanitary homes, and was responsible for a vast increase in the wealth and population of the country. But in the last half of the eighteenth century the great landowners and their tenants were unaware of any threat to England's "rural neatness and elegance".

The country house was affected by the prevailing fashions in architecture and furnishing. Many fine new houses were built, and Palladian additions—a new wing, a portico, or an entire frontage—were made to existing houses. The formal gardens of the seventeenth century were considered old-fashioned. ". . . Bridgeman and Kent—followed by Lancelot or 'Capability' Brown and Sir William Chambers—popularised an entirely different type of garden, one which aimed at reproducing the wildness of uncontrolled nature and which converted the garden into a luxuriant wilderness. One result of this new method was the introduction into the country of a greatly increased number of exotic varieties of shrubs and flowers, and a taste for botany was certainly encouraged."[1] Among the trees introduced was the larch.

The ideas of architects like Sir William Chambers were not without effect. In 1757 he published a book on *Designs of Chinese Buildings, Furniture, Dresses, Machines and Utensils*. His work illustrated the readiness and ability of the eighteenth-century architect to accept responsibility not only for the house and everything in it, but for the landscape too. Among the buildings he designed are Somerset House and the Albany in London. The pavilions, the orangery and the Chinese pagoda in Kew Gardens are his work, and they are examples of the varied ways of decorating grounds with graceful buildings. Hundreds of gardens had little classic temples, carefully placed to secure an ornamental effect in relation to trees and shrubs.

There was also another form of fashionable taste which touched

[1] *English Men and Manners in the Eighteenth Century*, by A. S. Turberville. Section XII, "The Artists", p. 358.

the grounds of the country house, and that was the affection for romantic ruins. On many estates there were the remains of mediaeval buildings, ruined chapels, fragments of church buildings that had survived from the early sixteenth century. These were made much of, and sometimes false ruins were deliberately built, and the fashion was even carried to the length of planting dead trees to give a mournful air to the mouldering tower or the tottering arch. As usual, the worst of these extravagances were known to the country folk as "follies", for their sturdy good sense always rebelled against such antics. Those men of the land often had glimpses of life as it was lived at the "big house", for the gardens which had formerly been enclosed by high brick walls, were sometimes partly opened to the public gaze by a hundred yards or so of fine wrought iron railings, generally put in to reveal some view over the fields and woods beyond the gardens.

It was through the owner of the large country house that changing fashions were made known and gradually introduced to the countryside. One of the results was that every type of home was better furnished, the cottage and the neat, compact houses of the professional men and the respectable traders who had retired to the country, and other people who were not rich but were comfortably off. Furniture in these small country homes now resembled the modish designs used in the great mansions. The country craftsmen still flourished—smiths, joiners, cabinet-makers, stone masons—and excellent local building work could be carried out with their help. The great tradition of skill in wood-working, which arose from the ancient partnership of forester, shipwright and builder in Saxon times, now bore its finest fruit, for the second half of the eighteenth century was the age of the great cabinet-makers. Such names as Chippendale, Ince, Mayhew, Hepplewhite, Shearer and Sheraton were associated with some of the finest furniture ever designed. It was in this period that the sideboard was perfected as a piece of furniture—long, bow-fronted or serpentine-fronted, it was one of the highest achievements of the cabinet-maker's craft.

A wealthy landowner would often commission a local cabinet-maker to copy some town-made article. In 1754, Thomas Chippendale had published a book which encouraged this practice: he called it *The Gentleman and Cabinet Maker's Director*. On the title page he described it as "a large collection of the most Elegant and Useful Designs of Household Furniture in the Gothic, Chinese and Modern Taste: Including a great Variety of Book-cases for Libraries or Private Rooms, Commodes, Library and Writing-Tables, Buroes, Breakfast-Tables, Dressing and China-Tables, China-Cases, Hanging-Shelves, Tea-Chests, Trays, Fire-Screens, Chairs, Settees, Sopha's, Beds, Presses and Cloaths-Chests, Pier-Glass Sconces, Slab Frames, Brackets, Candle-Stands, Clock-Cases, Frets, and other ornaments.

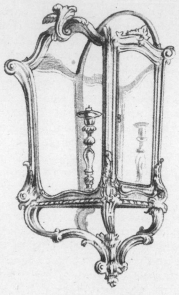

WALL LANTERN

A mid-eighteenth-century design which
should be compared with the earlier forms
shown on page 105.

The whole comprehended in One Hundred and Sixty Copper-Plates
neatly Engraved, Calculated to improve and refine the prefent Tafte
and fuited to the Fancy and Circumftances of Perfons in all Degrees
of Life.''

In a short preface, the author said that he had "given no design
but what may be executed with advantage by the hands of a skilled
workman . . .'' The impressive list of articles included in Chippendale's *Director* stimulated the skill of the country craftsman when,
at the squire's order, he made a new set of chairs for the dining room
of the "Hall", or tried his hand at one of the great architectural bookcases for the library. When he came to make things for humbler
homes, it was only natural that he should use some of the new
ideas he had gained. These skilful country workers had adopted the
once fashionable cabriole leg and used it on Windsor chairs; they
now adopted and simplified the ribbon-back and other modish
devices, and produced what was known as "Cottage Chippendale",
using elm, oak or beech instead of mahogany.

There were not only excellent copy books for the design of furniture, such as Chippendale's *Director*, Robert Manwaring's *Chair-
maker's Guide* and the volume on *Household Furniture* published by

W. Ince and J. Mayhew; there were many excellent books and collections of plates dealing with every detail of house building. The country builder was a good interpreter of the designs set forth in such works, but his ideas about the placing of a house on a site were rigid. In a town the front of a house and the best rooms nearly always faced the street, though there were some exceptions. For instance, a description of a moderately sized town house, written by a Bristol builder in 1724, makes it clear that it was undesirable to have some of the important rooms on the street front. "I think it an Error in people who make the Room where they eat, (which for many good reasons is generally avoided to be in the Front of the House where every Passenger looks in) less than what the same Company afterwards go only to sitt and converse in."[1] In the country the custom of making the front of the house face the road was generally followed, even though it might deprive the best rooms of sunlight. The small and moderately sized country house had to suggest grandeur, so the builder was compelled to present a trim and formal "front" to the roadway, and the custom remains to this day, except in a few garden cities and well-planned housing estates, where the individual houses or groups of houses are placed to the best advantage on the site. One effect of the universal use of architectural copybooks by country builders, was to destroy many local building customs, except in the smallest and simplest cottages.

Cottages were generally built in pairs, though sometimes a row of them, following on a small scale the idea of the terrace, would line part of a village street. The "pair" of cottages was the ancestor of the "semi-detached" house of to-day. All over the country well-proportioned comfortable houses were built, and, large or small, they had a good-mannered graciousness of aspect: the people who inhabited them liked to be comfortable, yet they desired an air of dignity. The rules for attaining both comfort and dignity had been set forth, printed, published and distributed to hundreds of builders. The latter part of the eighteenth century was the high noon of England's golden age of architecture.

"The prefent reign is indeed rendered remarkable by the multitude of magnificent buildings, fine ftreets, and fpacious fquares, that have been added, and ftill are adding to this metropolis," wrote the anonymous author of a six-volume work entitled *London and its Environs Described*, which was issued in 1761.[2] London had grown westwards as far as Park Lane, which was then called Tiburn Lane; northwards squares and gardens were being laid out, and the houses in them were tall, roomy and unpretentious. The regular spacing of the windows, which were sometimes taller on the first

[1] Quoted by Christopher Hussey in *Planning a House in 1724*, published in *Architectural Design and Construction*, Vol. I, No. 1, p. 25. November 1930.
[2] Printed for R. and J. Dodsley in Pall-Mall.

floor than on the ground floor and the upper storeys, the horizontal lines established by those rows of windows, the balustrading which often gave a finish to the coping above the top storey and concealed both the roof and the dormer windows of the attics, all combined to give an air of sober orderliness to those newly-built London squares and terraces. Only one feature marred this agreeable regularity of form and broke up the skyline of London and every other city: it appeared late in the eighteenth century, and was soon accepted as an inevitable accompaniment to house building: it was the chimney pot. Throughout the century there had been isolated examples of the use of funnels or cans, as they were called in Scotland, and in Cornwall the tops of chimneys were tapered in stone; but the development of housing schemes in London increased the number of flues that had to be carried up to the roof. Smoke issuing from one flue was often drawn downwards into another and smoky fire-places became an intolerable nuisance. A series of earthenware pots placed over the individual flues, where they came up through the brick chimney stack, guided the smoke upwards and improved the draught of the fire-place. But although these devices were used and accepted as necessary, architects generally ignored the fact that they would be added, and seldom made allowance for their height or attempted to incorporate them in the design of their buildings: so for years they were ragged after-thoughts that made the skyline untidy.

Brick was the chief building material used in town and country and its popularity was undiminished by a tax levied in 1784. On ordinary bricks, this tax was about 4s. 7d. per thousand, with a higher rate for special bricks: it was not repealed until 1850. Towards the end of the century stucco was used, at first only on town houses for facing the lower storey and for ornamental features. It was plastered on as a coat to the brickwork, and it provided a smooth surface for painting. This stucco facing was impressed with lines to imitate stone jointing. It was first introduced in England by the brothers Adam, those four talented Scotsmen, who coming from Edinburgh, which they had partly re-planned and rebuilt and where stone was cheap and plentiful, desired to obtain the effect of stonework in their London speculative building schemes.[1]

The brothers Adam had a profound influence upon fashionable taste in architecture and interior decoration and furnishing. This remarkable team of brains consisted of Robert, James and John Adam, who were architects, and William, a financial expert. Between them they had all the knowledge and training necessary for the planning and development of large-scale building schemes. Although Robert Adam had been appointed Architect to the King and the Board of

[1] *The Smaller English House of the Later Renaissance*, 1660–1830, by A. E. Richardson, F.S.A., F.R.I.B.A., and H. Donaldson Eberlein. Chap. III, p. 91.

LATE EIGHTEENTH-CENTURY INTERIOR

The brothers Adam had a great influence upon taste in architecture, interior decoration and furnishing in the latter part of the eighteenth century. They were prepared and able to design anything, from elegant chairs and sideboards, mirrors, chandeliers and candlesticks, to great housing schemes like Portland Place and the Adelphi in London. All their work was based on classic architectural forms and ornament.

Works in 1762, he resigned from that post after six years and gave his entire time to speculative building. The brothers acquired some derelict property by the Thames south of the Strand, and built a great block of buildings, high above the quays. They called it the Adelphi. "Here the occupants lived as if on a rock without being disturbed by the warehouse traffic below. The cellars ran 265 feet into the obscure underworld below the buildings and streets."[1] The brothers nearly ruined themselves in this speculation, but a lottery was sanctioned by Parliament, and individual houses in the Adelphi were offered as prizes. Other building schemes in London designed by the gifted partnership, include two sides of Fitzroy Square, Portland Place, and Stratford Place in Oxford Street.

There had been a revival of taste for classic architecture, partly due to the immense interest aroused by the excavation and published descriptions of the buried Roman cities of Pompeii and Herculaneum. Robert Adam had spent some time in Dalmatia, surveying the ruins of Diocletian's palace at Salonae, and in 1764 he published an illustrated description of the ruins, with plates by Bartolozzi. He was well equipped to satisfy the fashionable demand for correct classical detail in architecture; and he designed houses with a completeness that left little scope for the expression of the owner's personal taste.

In the second half of that century of many fashions, two vastly different forms of taste, Chinese and Gothic, had considerable influence on the shape of furniture and the interior treatment of houses. In the Queen Anne and early Georgian periods, Chinese lacquer furniture, porcelain and painted wall papers had been popular; by the middle years of the century the collection of oriental objects had become a craze and Chinese ornaments and patterns appeared everywhere. Curtain materials and chair coverings, wall papers and furniture in "the Chinese taste" adorned the rooms of the large town house. Chippendale's Chinese designs included chairs with lattice backs in imitation of Chinese fretwork, mirror frames wreathed about with dragons and the figures of Chinese warriors, and cabinets and hanging shelves in the form of pagodas, complete in every detail, even to the little soundless bells of carved and gilded wood, dangling from every set of eaves. These extravagances of fashion were seldom ill-proportioned or clumsy or badly-made; the taste of society was still highly educated, and gentlemen believed, in the words of Gibbon, that "the practice of architecture is directed by a few general and even mechanical rules". They were familiar with those rules.

The taste for Gothic architecture followed a growing interest in antiquarian studies, and most enthusiastic of antiquaries was Horace Walpole, whose villa at Strawberry Hill, near Twickenham, became

---

[1] *London: The Unique City*, by Steen Eiler Rasmussen. Chap. IX, p. 179.

the most striking example of this architectural revival. He described it as "a little plaything-house"; it might well have been called "plaything-Gothic". As an antiquary "he was enthusiastic, ignorant, full of amateurish and improbable theories," writes Mr. Ketton-Cremer in his biography of this eccentric but gifted nobleman who exerted such a far-reaching influence on taste and fashion in architecture. He gives a compact and excellent picture of the sources of Walpole's romantic love for Gothic buildings. "All over England stood the ruined monasteries and castles, neglected, crumbling, turned into cottages and cowsheds and quarries for building. One pushed through the nettles and skirted the duckponds, thrust aside a hurdle and entered the chapel or the refectory of a great monastic house. One rode or drove through almost impassable lanes, and came upon historic mansions tumbling in ruin, with paint still visible on their carvings, painted glass in their windows, and perhaps a farm labourer's family shivering in one of the towers. One traced forgotten cloisters, detected the site of kitchens and high altars, stood in great undercrofts whose forests of pillars glistened with water; one found the castle well and the castle privies, and made unlikely speculations about the tiltyard and the ladye's bower; and returned to the inn inspired with the romance of the past."[1]

Walpole had been a frequent visitor at the beautiful house at Sherborne St. John in Hampshire, called the Vyne, which was the home of his friend, John Chute. Like many great country houses, it was an harmonious blend of ancient and contemporary building; the late fifteenth- and early sixteenth-century parts, with their Gothic flavour, the new portico built in accordance with Roman rules, rearing its Corinthian columns to the roof line and crowned by a massive pediment; the smiling sash windows of the Georgian period inserted in the pale, rose-coloured Tudor brickwork with its criss-cross patterns of purple-blue vitreous headers—all these happily related features and materials must have continually suggested to the impressionable amateur of architecture how well two vastly different styles could be associated.

More than one architect thought it was possible to regularise Gothic architecture, and in 1747, Batty Langley had published a book on *Gothic Architecture, Improved by Rules and Proportions, in many Grand Designs of Columns, Doors, Windows, Chimney-pieces, Arcades, Colonades, Porticoes, Umbrellos, Temples and Pavilions, etc., with Plans, Elevations and Profiles, Geometrically Expressed*. According to Horace Walpole, all that Batty Langley's books on the subject achieved "has been to teach carpenters to massacre that venerable species . . ." Walpole could write of his satisfaction "in imprinting the gloomth of abbeys and cathedrals on one's house. . . ." But although he had no intention or desire to lead fashion in Gothic

[1] *Horace Walpole*, by R. W. Ketton-Cremer. Chap. VII, pp. 135–136.

taste, and was concerned only with the furnishing and decoration of his own house, "Strawberry Hill Gothic" was imitated by builders and designers of furniture. The glazing bars in the upper parts of sash windows were curved to form a trio of pointed arches: those arches were woven into chair backs and the glazed doors of bookcases and cabinets. But such Gothic forms were neatly fitted into the framework of good architectural design: they were, until the next century, regarded chiefly as a means of ornament.

In town houses ornamentation became lighter and more graceful. New architectural features were introduced which helped to increase the effect of lightness and delicacy. It has been said that "windows are eyes of buildings; they are either demure and modest, forward and leering, stern and official, or delicate and inviting."[1] The bow window was now used, swelling out in a gentle curve from the front of a house, ascending to the second storey, beautifully proportioned and usually built entirely of wood. Bay windows of wood also became common in small town and country houses. The glazing bars of the sashes were much thinner, and this increased the amount of light admitted to rooms. Narrow wrought iron balconies appeared at each window of the first floor and sometimes extended to the full width of the house. At the end of the century trellised verandah balconies were used, but were generally confined to houses in fashionable spas and seaside resorts.

Area railings, door lanterns and link extinguishers were more fancifully and elaborately designed, and the front door itself became most impressive and dignified. Its width and importance increased; on either side pilasters supported an entablature, or columns upheld a protecting roof to form a stately porch. Sometimes an unsupported canopy was designed in the form of an inverted shell; sometimes a little sheltering roof was bracketed forward, with a fanlight above it to admit light to the hall. Fanlights were delicate pieces of tracery in wood or metal.

After entering a house in the fashionable quarters of London, the astonishing abundance of furniture and ornaments would impress the country visitor, for fashionable folk lived with a tremendous sense of style. The various rooms were lofty and were designed to form an appropriate background for people; and as the ladies and gentlemen who used them were most decorative, the extreme delicacy of late eighteenth-century interiors and the pale colouring on the walls, were in agreeable contrast with their rich and glittering clothes. In houses designed by the brothers Adam, walls and ceilings were covered with raised decoration, copied originally from antique models, but used with copious invention and carried out in hard plaster and painted. The marble chimney-pieces were in

[1] *The Smaller English House of the Later Renaissance*, 1660–1830, by A. E. Richardson, F.S.A., F.R.I.B.A., and H. Donaldson Eberlein. Chap. III, p. 147.

A STREET IN A FASHIONABLE SPA, REGENCY PERIOD.

themselves complete compositions, with columns and entablatures, so that the mantelpiece had the dignity of some temple portico. The iron hob grate was cast with ornament that matched the character of the plasterwork. Soft, pastel colours were used on walls and painted furniture: a shade of green, that is still known as Adam's green, powder and turquoise blues, dusty pinks, greys, pale ochre, cream and stone, strengthened occasionally by some deeper hue, such as terra cotta or a Pompeian red. The lines of these rooms were softened by curves: arches and dome-topped niches were introduced, and sometimes one end of the room would be oval.

Such fashionable foreign artists as Cipriani, Pergolesi, Zucchi and his wife Angelica Kauffmann, were often employed to paint panels and ceilings in rooms designed by Robert Adam. Furniture placed in these rooms was designed to harmonise with the decoration. The same ornamental devices were used: floral and leafy swags, ram's heads, festoons of drapery and sheaves of corn tied with flowing knots of ribbon. The furniture was light and simple in form, with tapering legs on chairs and tables, and it was made of mahogany and sometimes of satinwood. The artists employed to paint ceilings and wall panels, often painted decoration on furniture.

The Englishman's Castle, whether in town or country, was a most elegant and agreeable place in the closing years of the century. Many crafts and industries contributed things of beauty to the furnishing of homes. English glass had become famous; goldsmiths and silversmiths were superbly skilled craftsmen, and the silver ware of this time is among some of the finest ever produced; silk weaving flourished, both at Spitalfields and at Braintree; china and pottery were growing from small, simple country crafts into great industries, producing decorative and household ware of the highest order. No longer was it necessary for the collector to fill his shelves exclusively with exotic wares from the Orient: Chelsea, Fulham, Worcester, Derby, Bow, and, most famous of all, the new Wedgwood works at Etruria, near Hanley, were all hard at work—building up England's great reputation for fine pottery. Josiah Wedgwood had as great an influence upon the design and character of English pottery as Inigo Jones had upon architecture. His epitaph in the parish church of Stoke-on-Trent records that he "converted a rude and inconsiderable Manufactory into an elegant Art and an important part of National Commerce." He was born in 1730 and died in 1795. Although he perfected such famous decorative products as the pale, cream-coloured "Queen's Ware," which was first produced for Queen Charlotte in 1765, his earliest work was the improvement of domestic ware. He was concerned with "the invention of new bodies and material, colours, and new methods of manufacture. His tortoise-shell, agate, mottled, and other coloured pieces were distinct creations. . . . He supplemented the use of the primitive potter's wheel by afterwards turning his ware upon an improved lathe. He was the actual inventor of at least twenty new bodies for the manufacture of earthenware, many of which are in use to this day by all potters."[1] It was found that English clay was suitable for making the finest pastes, and that the English potter had a particular genius and aptitude for his work. Everywhere on tea tables in town drawing-rooms, on the dressers and mantelshelves of cottage kitchens, on the small mahogany washstands in bedrooms, gay colours and bold or delicate patterns appeared on cups and saucers, bowls, jugs, basins and drinking mugs.

Cooking, heating and lighting methods remained unchanged, though the design of fire-places, grates, candelabra and chandeliers varied according to fashion. Crystal chandeliers, holding a score or more of candles, were used, and wall lights with two or three arms had backs of mirror to double the power of their candles.

Kitchens were large, spacious rooms in which the enormous quantity of dishes and side dishes, which formed the meals of the period, were efficiently cooked. The floors were mostly of stone flags. The huge open fire-place, with hooks for kettles and stewpots, had as its central fixture, a spit upon which the meat was roasted. This spit was moved by means of jacks and was made to revolve slowly during cooking so that all sides of the joint were evenly browned. Below it on the hearth were two long shallow trays to catch the fat as it sizzled off the cooking meat. Plain wooden shelves held an array of cooking pots of iron or copper, and from the rafters were hung sides of bacon, ham and other smoked meats, great bunches of onions and knots of pot herbs. Brick ovens, generally heated by wood, were also in use, but they were kept entirely for baking pies, bread and pastry. No large country house was complete without its cool stone-flagged dairy, its larders big enough to hang game in season, and its still-room for storing all the varieties of preserved foods which were made from the produce of the gardens and orchards. Even the smaller houses were thus equipped, though on a lesser scale, for it was an age of abundant food, grown and dressed for and by the family.

Those who worked in the kitchens of the big country houses, in farmhouses or cottages, were better off than those who drudged in the town; for even the fine new houses built in the Adelphi contained dark basements where the servants lived. Kitchens were driven underground in the town, whether the house was large or small.

Improvements in sanitation had been made, and in 1775 the first valve water closet was patented by Alexander Cummings, and

[1] *A Catalogue of the Wedgwood Museum, Etruria,* by Frederick Rathbone. "Biographical Notes", p.16.

SMOKER'S SET IN STEEL, ABOUT 1790

During the Georgian period the design of nearly every article had elegance as well as functional fitness.

before the end of the century water closets had been installed in a few town and country houses. Sewage disposal was still primitive; the night carts still collected slop pails from town houses, though the new water closets drained into sealed tanks called cesspools, which were shared by two or more houses, and sometimes by a terrace. They were buried well below ground level, and cleared out periodically.

The water supply improved in London, and the Chelsea Water Company was in operation, piping Thames water to houses, as early as 1721. The Lambeth waterworks were erected in 1783. But wells were still the chief source of supply: a common pump would serve a terrace or a court in the town, or a group of cottages in a village.

Although its equipment may, from the modern point of view, have been defective and inconvenient; although the comfort and health of servants were largely ignored, the eighteenth-century house was a beautiful and well-ordered home. The architects of that age set a standard for house building in town and country, which had never before been attained, and has not yet been surpassed.

CHAPTER XIV

THE GOLDEN AGE OF BUILDING
ENDS
(A.D. 1800–1850)

GEORGIAN architecture and all the gracious ways of life and elegant fashions for which it had formed a perfect background came to an end in the first third of the nineteenth century. It was succeeded by a period of confusion and vulgarity in building, for the taste of the nobility and gentry and the new prosperous middle class became first romantic and then coarse. Educated judgment in matters of architecture was rare. Instead of being magnificent, large houses were merely pretentious. The orderliness that had distinguished the plan and the appearance of the Georgian home at last disappeared. In no other century of English history had so many drastic changes occurred in the homes of every class. There were many improvements, but they were improvements in materials and apparatus. The design of houses and furniture disimproved as elegance gave way to respectability.

The towns were enormously enlarged. In the Midlands and the North thousands of houses were built in mean streets, back-to-back, without gardens, without proper water supply or sanitation, so that their inhabitants, dwelling beneath the ever-deepening smoke-cloud of nineteenth-century industrialism, lived in unspeakable squalor. The slave quarters of the Roman villa-house, the wattle-and-daub huts of Saxon serfs and mediaeval villeins, were better than dank brick boxes, designed and built by greed. Only the very cheapest materials were used. Bricks, far inferior in quality to those normally employed, were set in the poorest mortar. Had timber been available, it might have formed the principal material for those houses; but the timber houses which had been built in many parts of the south country and in East Anglia were not copied in the industrial towns; the demands of the Royal Navy upon wood supplies during the Napoleonic wars had been vast and continuous, and there was little timber to spare for building complete houses. The new, excessively cheap bricks that were made in millions, could compete in price with weather-boarding, so no more pleasant wooden houses were built after the beginning of the century.[1]

These hideous extensions to towns and cities came upon England unawares. While row after row of back-to-back houses were being built for the men, women and children employed in factories,

[1] *Timber Houses*, edited by E. H. B. Boulton. Introduction, p. 9.

authors like Felicia Dorothea Hemans could write romantically about the "Homes of England". She dwelt not only on the charms of great houses: she also gave attention to the cottage, as the first and fourth verses of her famous poem indicate:

"The stately homes of England,
How beautiful they stand!
Amidst their tall ancestral trees,
O'er all the pleasant land!
The deer across the greenwood bound,
Through shade and sunny gleam;
And the swan glides past them with the sound
Of some rejoicing stream.

"The cottage homes of England!
By thousands, on her plains,
They are smiling o'er her silvery brooks,
And round the hamlet fanes.
Through glowing orchards forth they peep,
Each from its mote of leaves,
And fearless there they lowly sleep,
As the bird beneath their eaves."

There was truth in those praises of the cottage homes. The country folk lived in cottages that were still soundly built from local materials; the gracious simplicity of the eighteenth century survived in those small buildings. Sometimes pointed arches appeared in door and window openings, generally when new cottages were erected by a landlord whose taste had been influenced by the great and growing interest in the architecture of the Middle Ages, which fostered the Gothic revival. Horace Walpole's hobby of Gothic architecture at Strawberry Hill had been raised to much higher levels of extravagance by James Wyatt, who designed Fonthill Abbey in the closing years of the eighteenth century for that wealthy, accomplished and most eccentric man of taste, William Beckford. This enormous, sham-Gothic building, which rose high above the woodlands of a fine estate in Wiltshire, did not survive. A few years after Beckford had sold the house, the huge tower, which was 260 feet high, collapsed and wrecked part of the building. Altogether, Beckford spent some £273,000 on Fonthill.

The taste for Gothic architecture was certainly encouraged by the works of Sir Walter Scott. People thought with excitement and pleasure of the "romance" and "chivalry" of the Middle Ages. They forgot or ignored what was happening under their eyes in England. With the help of Sir Walter, they shuddered about mediaeval dungeons, but knew little or nothing about the slums that were housing the new, neglected class of factory workers. They preferred "the good old times" to the troubles and problems of their own times; and this taste for old ideas at last marked the appearance and contents of their houses. The nobility was particularly delighted with mediaeval ways, and on August 28th and 29th, 1839, a tournament was held by Lord Eglintoun at Eglintoun Castle in Scotland. There were lists and many gay pavilions; banners bearing heraldic devices floated above the heads of thousands of spectators; heralds, pursuivants, halberdiers, men-at-arms and splendidly equipped knights enlivened the scene. Lady Seymour was enthroned as the Queen of Beauty. It was like a chapter from *Ivanhoe*. But in Scott's romances the weather was usually fine: this occasion was sobered by steady rain.

Fashion was growing foolish. The Roman rules had been good guides to the architects of the golden age of English building, though to their originators they had been iron-handed tyrants. Gothic ideas were neither guides nor tyrants; they were like drugs; they caused architects and their patrons to lose all sense of harmony and order: anarchy in design naturally followed. "The battle of the styles" began. During the nineteenth century the classic and Gothic styles were in conflict, some architects favouring one, some the other; a few building happily in either style, like Sir Charles Barry, who, assisted by Pugin, designed the Houses of Parliament. But for the first half of the century country life took no account of this fashion war: it was still pleasant and reasonably prosperous, serene and untroubled.

In the eighteen-twenties, William Cobbett, thundering forth advice, criticism and praise, set down many fears about new-fangled ideas that threatened the simple ways of cottagers. He was particularly severe on the habit of tea drinking, which had now spread to all classes. Writing in his *Cottage Economy*, which he issued in monthly parts during 1821, he said:

"It is notorious, that tea has no *useful strength* in it; that it contains nothing *nutricious*; that it, besides being *good* for nothing, has *badness* in it, because it is well known to produce want of sleep in many cases, and, in all cases, to shake and weaken the nerves. It is, in fact, a weaker kind of laudanum, which enlivens for the moment, and deadens afterwards. At any rate it communicates no strength to the body; it does not, in any degree, assist in affording what labour demands. It is then, of no *use*." Cobbett estimated that tea drinking in the course of a year amounted to "a good third part of a good and able labourer's wages."

Cobbett's belief that household goods should be *warm*, *strong* and *durable* made him condemn some of the convenient household things that were made in factories. He held that the equipment of the cottage should be handed on from generation to generation, and it often was, for before the craze for collecting antique furniture began early in the twentieth century, "the cottage homes of England" were well equipped with furniture of oak and beech and elm—

FOUR CENTURIES OF HOUSE BUILDING AT DARTMOUTH

Brick and plaster, sash windows and casements, Tudor and Georgian doorways, are found side by side in hundreds of old English streets. Sometimes the use of one particular material would give a family likeness to houses built in different centuries. (See page 142.)

fine examples of the country cabinet-maker's work. "As to bedding, and other things of that sort," said Cobbett, "all ought to be good in their nature, of a durable quality, and plain in their colour and form. The plates, dishes, mugs, and things of that kind, should be of *pewter*, or even of wood. Bottles to carry a-field should be of wood. Formerly, nobody but the gipseys and mumpers, that went a hop-picking in the season, carried glass or earthern bottles. As to *glass* of any sort, I do not know, what business it has in any man's house, unless he be rich enough to live on his means. It pays a tax, in many cases, to the amount of two-thirds of its cost. In short, when a house is once furnished with sufficient goods, there ought to be no renewal of hardly any part of them wanted for half an age, except in case of destruction by fire."

Many large country houses were built in the opening years of the century, and these were still designed in accordance with the taste for Roman and Greek architecture. Stucco, used first by the brothers Adam to simulate stonework and confined to the lower storey of a building, was now spread all over the brickwork so that houses with smooth walls painted white, cream or buff, rose amid their gardens—cool, comfortable and spacious.

In the towns; streets, crescents and circuses were built in this new style of classic architecture which developed early in the century, during the Regency. The chief leader in this form of architectural taste was John Nash, the Prince Regent's architect. He was the last English architect whose designs controlled and influenced the development of large sections of London and other cities and towns. The tall, pale coloured stucco houses of the Regency period altered the appearance of Brighton and Hove, Tenby, Leamington, Cheltenham and many other places. In London, one of the finest examples of Nash's work is Regent's Park, with its terraces and crescents.

Although those delicately proportioned stucco buildings have since been admired, they were compared unfavourably with brickwork at the time they were built. A verse appeared in the *Quarterly Review* in 1826 criticising the style that Nash had popularised:

> "Augustus at Rome was for building renown'd,
> And of marble he left what of brick he had found;
> But is not our Nash, too, a very great master?
> He finds us all brick and he leaves us all plaster."[1]

The new houses in the fashionable watering places did not always satisfy popular ideas of comfort and cosiness. All kinds and conditions of people went to Brighton, which the Prince of Wales had turned into a centre of fashion. He lived at the Pavilion, an agree-

[1] *Quarterly Review*, XXXIV, 1826, p. 193. John Summerson in quoting this in his biography of *John Nash*, suggests that "this was evidently not its first appearance in print". Chap. VII, p. 138.

SEASIDE TOWN HOUSE, EARLY NINETEENTH CENTURY.

ably proportioned house, transformed into an elaborate oriental structure. "It is good in parts; tiresome and clumsy in others. The building was its owner's private toy, not a public building, like Buckingham Palace, and the Prince was under no obligation to please anyone but himself. His architect was merely the instrument of his whims."[1]

While the Prince and his circle of friends amused themselves at the Pavilion, more ordinary people who were trying to be fashionable regretted the comforts they had left behind them, when they spent Christmas at Brighton.

> "Our register-stoves and our crimson-baized doors,
> Our weather-proof walls, and our carpeted floors,
> Our casements, well fitted to stem the north wind,
> Our arm-chair and sofa, are all left behind.
> We lodge on the Steine, in a bow-window'd box,
> That beckons up stairs every zephyr that knocks;
> The sun hides his head and the elements frown;
> But nobody now spends his Christmas in Town."[2]

The "bow window'd box" could be comfortable; it contained high, well-lit rooms of good proportion, and its appearance was handsome, particularly when it formed part of a long terrace. The smooth surface of the stucco facing, with its unbroken sweep of pale coloured paint, the replacement of cornices by plain, slightly projecting bands, and the restrained use of ornament all helped to create an effect of simplicity. Cast iron was used instead of wrought iron for railings and balconies; it was then one of the latest materials and was employed with great skill. Verandahs of cast iron shaded the ground floor rooms of many Regency country houses, and after 1820 semi-circular ribbed window canopies of the same material were often used on the upper floors above shallow bay windows. Thin glazing bars still divided sash windows into twelve or more rectangular panes; and the french window, which was really a glazed door, was introduced.

Roofs were no longer steep in pitch; slate was used frequently instead of tile, and in many Regency houses the roof was flat. But architects still seemed to think that their responsibility for the outside appearance of the house stopped at the chimney stacks. In the new town houses, large or small, flues were often badly designed, so directly a building was up the chimney stacks were crowned with pots that grew taller and taller until in the eighteen-forties the zinc "tallboy" brought fresh disfigurement to the roofs of London and other cities. When Mr. Pickwick remarked upon the delightful prospect of the countryside seen from a coach top, no wonder Sam Weller replied: "Beats the chimley pots, sir."

[1] *John Nash*, by John Summerson, Chap. IX, p. 159.
[2] *New Monthly Magazine*, 1825.

PARK CRESCENT, REGENT'S PARK, BY JOHN NASH

Classic architecture gained new beauty from the use of stucco, which was spread over the brickwork of houses, giving them smooth walls which were painted white, cream or buff.

The flues of the larger houses were so rambling and complicated, that they could not be swept without the assistance of small boys, who were apprenticed to chimney sweeps and whose duty was to climb up the chimneys and brush out the soot. These apprentices were occasionally suffocated.

Many speculative builders, whose work was undirected by a competent architect, began to build cheaply and badly with the sole object of making as much money as possible with the least effort. These men, without pride or skill, were the fathers of jerry-building. John Nash, himself a renowned speculative builder, but also an architect of genius and a business man with a conscience, deplored this growing menace in one of his reports to the Commissioners of Woods and Forests. He said: ". . . the artificial causes of the extension of the town are the speculation of builders, encouraged and promoted by merchants dealing in the materials of building, and of attorneys with monied clients facilitating and, indeed, putting in motion the whole system, by disposing of their client's money in premature mortgages, the sale of improved ground rents and by numerous other devices. . . . It is not necessary for the present purpose to enumerate the bad consequences and pernicious effects which arise from such unnatural and enforced enlargements of the town, further than to observe, that it is the interest of those concerned in such buildings that they should be of as little cost as possible preserving an attractive exterior, which Parker's stucco, coloured bricks and balconies accomplish; and a fashionable arrangement of rooms on the principal floors embellished by the paper hanger and a few flimsy marble chimney pieces are the attractions of the interior. These are sufficient allurements to the public, and ensure the sale of the house, which is the ultimate object of the builders; and to this finery everything out of sight is sacrificed, or, is no further an object of attention, *than, that no defects in the constructive and substantial parts make their appearance while the houses are on sale*; and it is to be feared that for want of these essentials which constitute the strength and permanency of houses, a very few years will exhibit crooked walls, swagged floors, bulging fronts, crooked roofs, leaky gutters, inadequate drains and other ills of an originally bad constitution; and it is quite certain, without a renovation equal to rebuilding, that all these houses, long, very long, before the expiration of the leases, will cease to exist. ...."[1]

A new and ignorant public was ready to be cheated: they accepted jerry-building because it looked genteel, and all they cared about was the outward appearance of a house. They lacked the critical knowledge of the eighteenth-century nobility and gentry. The large town houses, whether they were designed by architects, or were run up by jerry-builders, had many defects of planning. The principal rooms might be spacious and elegantly appointed, but the servants' quarters were dark and rambling, and the comfort of domestic workers was ignored throughout the century. There were plenty of servants, they worked for small wages, and were apparently prepared to endure the discomfort and unnecessary work that arose from faulty planning. Every article in domestic equipment was made on the assumption that abundant labour would be available for cleaning it, and the idea of labour-saving finishes for such things as grates and stoves never occurred either to manufacturers or users.

Many new domestic appliances were being introduced. The open kitchen hearth with its roasting spit and brick baking ovens was being replaced in up-to-date homes by what was called a "patent kitchener", made of cast iron. It consisted of a raised central fire retained by bars, and flanked by two roasting and baking ovens. Over the ovens and fire was a hot plate, surmounted by two clumsy, box-like flues. This type of range was the ancestor of the modern labour-saving and efficient kitchen cooker, and it marks the first big and radical change in cooking methods since the earliest times. By 1829 these patent kitcheners were to be found in all the new houses, and they were also being installed in older houses. Some of them were equipped with a primitive water-heating system.

Candles still served as the chief form of lighting, although oil-burning lamps were often used in the principal rooms of the house. Gas lighting was first introduced in 1807, when Pall Mall was illuminated by the new method. The Chartered Gas Light and Coke Company was formed in 1812, and before 1816 many streets in

[1] Quoted in *Metropolitan Improvements*, by Thomas H. Shepherd, introductory chapter, p. 8.

Westminster and London were gas lit. The new method of lighting was only gradually adopted for houses. It was quite the most revolutionary change that had taken place in the English home. Those little hot jets of flame sprouting from adapted chandeliers, which were called gaseliers, and from innumerable wall brackets, lacked the soft honey-coloured light of the fine wax candle.

Plumbing was greatly improved, and although bathrooms were rare, water-closets were now included in new houses. It was during the eighteen-thirties that sanitation was first recognised as a public responsibility. "Between 1830–1840 drainage from large houses in London was diverted through sewers into the Thames, which became a vast cesspool. When it is realised that the main water supply to the City of London was drawn from the Thames in those days, it is scarcely surprising that disease was rife. Drains were built of stone or porous brick or were simply open sewers, thus adding to the evil. There were visitations of plague, typhoid fever and cholera, which took dread toll of the congested populations not only of London but of other cities and towns where conditions were even worse. In 1842, a noted engineer, Edwin Chadwick, issued a report on public sanitation which so decisively exposed these and other scandals that a Commission on the Health of Towns was set up the following year. Local legislation followed and in 1848 the first Public Health Act was passed."[1]

Outwardly, houses did not change much between 1820 and 1840: they continued the modes of the Regency period. They were a little heavier; everything was thicker, foreshadowing the love of solidity, of mass and weight, which was presently to characterise the Victorian home. It was in the country that the romantic style of building developed, and it produced such creations as the *cottage ornée*.

A retired man of business might live in such a dwelling; but more often they were built on some large country estate, as an ornament to a romantic landscape, and for use as a summer pavilion, or as a home for a head keeper or some other estate servant. Taste in landscape gardening favoured the introduction of a small, picturesque cottage. The 'downward drooping eaves, the twisted chimneys and steeply pitched roofs and gables, the walls smothered in creepers and climbing shrubs, gave these cottages a shaggy appearance. They seemed like dwelling places for some character out of the popular German romances of the time, a woodcutter's daughter or a charcoal burner, rather than for the country folk or solid City merchants for whom they were built. In the country towns the tradespeople and professional folk lived in small, neat stucco villas which looked, and were, extremely comfortable.

During the Regency period, English furniture was influenced by

[1] *Official Architect*, Vol. 4, No. 4, April 1941. "Sanitation Through the Ages", by Desmond Eyles.

French taste. Napoleon had become regal: he liked his surroundings to suggest the pomp and magnificence of a Caesar, and the result was the classical French Empire style. Furniture that had been made in bronze and stone in Roman times was copied and elaborated in mahogany and marble with gilded bronze embellishments. The English version of such furniture was called English Empire. It was graceful in shape, but was heavily burdened with ornament. Mahogany, satinwood and rosewood were used, with elaborate brass inlays; and many articles were painted and gilded.

Furniture was now greatly varied in form and function. From 1820 to 1850 it grew heavy in design; good proportion was lost; carved ornament was clumsy and upholstery was bloated. The rooms in which this furniture appeared usually had papered walls. Regency wall papers were marbled in rich tones. In large houses walls were often covered with stretched brocade or damask. Brocade was used for window curtains, also plain, heavy Roman satin, serge, twill, velvet and merino. Soft muslins were used for looped inner curtains, and tie-backs for the outer and inner curtains made their first appearance. Colours were rather sombre during the Regency period: deep claret red, Imperial purple, dark green, many shades of brown and maroon, deep cream enriched with gold, light turquoise blue and Pompeian red, were all used. From 1820 onwards the colours were much brighter, the reds sharper, the purples harsh instead of soft and rich, and the blues metallic and staring.

A magazine, called *Ackerman's Repository of Arts, Literature, Commerce, Manufacture, Fashion, and Politics*, published regularly during the early years of the century, had from time to time, coloured illustrations of furniture accompanied by descriptive matter under the heading "Fashionable Furniture". Every number of this magazine carried a page on which were pasted small samples of actual material, both for dress and furnishing. A typical example of popular furnishing is illustrated in the number for April 1811. This shows a plain, single bed set against a wall with the most imposing draped canopy supported by projecting, heavy gilt spears. The drapery is a bright, sharp blue lined with white and trimmed with heavy gold fringe and braid. It is described as "The military couch bed, forms two elegant pieces of furniture, both useful and ornamental, and cannot but be a most desirable article for every family of distinction. A couch bed on this plan, which may be made in almost a thousand different forms, and in any style of fashion, is one of the most complete accommodations it is possible for any upholsterer to invent, for a second drawing room, dressing room, etc. A further description is scarcely necessary, the drawing explains itself: it may be made highly ornamental, or in a more plain and neat manner." That was the trouble in the early nineteenth century: only too often was the upholsterer allowed to invent the "thousand

ROW OF HOUSES AT CHIPPING CAMPDEN, 1450 TO 1850

Despite variations in style, the use of local stone and local building methods give unity to this street. (See page 135.)

different forms", only too seldom was he content to work in "a more plain and neat manner".

Gradually the furnishing of homes large or small, became a process of accumulating a vast collection of objects, ornamental, useful and useless. The correct taste of the eighteenth-century householder would have been shocked by the number of ill-designed, unhappily ornamented things that were crowded into rooms.

Englishmen of all classes loved their homes, and although the inhabitants of a couple of rooms in one of the back-to-back houses in the slums of Sheffield, Leeds, Birmingham or Manchester, had little reason to love the hovel where they lived, yet the word "home" meant much to them: they resented being turned out, as they frequently were, for non-payment of rent. Everywhere improvements were being made in methods and materials for building; generally they were misused. The whole land was changing. The forests had practically disappeared two hundred years before; now the countryside itself was threatened. No estate was safe, no landowner could be certain that on the borders of his park some factory would not gush smoke into the air. The stage coach gave place to the railway. All rural areas near an industrial town were begrimed, and when a once-clear river reached such a town it was polluted. The progress of the river through the mid-nineteenth-century town was thus described by Charles Kingsley:

> "Dank and foul, dank and foul,
>   By the smoky town in its murky cowl;
> Foul and dank, foul and dank,
>   By wharf and sewer and slimy bank;
> Darker and darker the farther I go,
> Baser and baser the richer I grow . . ."

142

But even in the darkened streets of the towns thousands of windows were gay with miniature gardens, for the window-box, with its few sooty plants, often represented the poor townsman's only contact with nature. Towards the middle of the century he had another; for the aspidistra was introduced, and from its cultivation arose the queer, snobbish legend that every flourishing leaf of the plant represented a hundred pounds of a family's annual income.

Although he was becoming a specialist in solid comfort, it could still be said that above all other things the Englishman demanded privacy. To quote "A Sketch of National Character" published in the *European Review* during 1825: "His own mind is the castle of his opinions, into which it would be as great a crime for you to break, as it would be for one not having a legal warrant to break into the castle of his house. Even in the construction of that house, you find evidence of that power which loosens him from all other matters, and binds him to himself; for, however inconvenient it may be for his weighty self, and his weightier spouse, to waddle up and down half a dozen flights of trap stairs, he will consent to have no family either in the floor above him, or in the floor under him. Be the house large or small, palace, or pile of chip-boxes, he must, when he goes out, be able to lock the door, and put the key in his pocket; and when he is in, there must be nothing about the pile, save the earth, the Englishman and the sky."

CHAPTER XV

THE VICTORIAN HOME
(A.D. 1850–1900)

IKE the Elizabethans before them, the Victorians had an appetite for profusion. The country was again dominated not only by a new rich class, but by newly created wealth. Industrial development brought immense riches to the nation, and once again the English, because of their industry and shipping, found themselves, to repeat a quotation made earlier, "competitors for the domination of the earth". Again it could be said "no wonder that their hearts distended with pride, and, hardening in their strength, gloried. A new sense of exaltation possessed the country, the exaltation of knowledge and power."[1]

The exultant belief in their country, in progress and in themselves, made the Victorians demand magnificence; but they also demanded comfort, and the result was ostentation. The Elizabethans had little sense of comfort, but they had a sense of fitness and an eye for beauty. The Victorians parted with all sense of fitness, and the houses of the rich resembled the Stuart houses of the early seventeenth century, and could be described in much the same words. Everything was overdone; everything was complicated by a vulgar profusion of carving and embellishment; every article sagged under masses of ornament. Taste had thickened.[2] Simplicity was confused with poverty; good proportion in architecture was neither understood nor recognised; and so far as the visual arts were concerned, England became a country of the blind.

Architecture ceased to express the needs of life: the love of picturesque effects, the romantic taste for Gothic, and the writings of John Ruskin all helped to confuse the ideas of the nobility, the gentry and the new, aggressively prosperous middle classes. Houses were no longer designed with an eye to good proportion: they were put into fancy dress—something old or something foreign. Ruskin, who hated the orderly beauty of classic architecture, urged people to destroy its harmonious effects by adding Gothic features and oddments of ornament to their houses. "Do not be afraid of incongruities," he said; "do not think of unities of effect. Introduce your Gothic line by line and stone by stone; never mind mixing it with your present architecture; your existing houses will be none the worse for having little bits of better work fitted to them; build a porch, or point a window, if you can do nothing else; and remember

[1] *The English Voyages of the Sixteenth Century*, by Sir Walter Raleigh. Quoted on p. 61.
[2] See p. 73.

THE ENGLAND THAT DICKENS DESCRIBED: THE EIGHT BELLS, HATFIELD.

that it is the glory of Gothic architecture that it can do *anything*."[1]
Many people and some architects thought it could do everything,
and as artistic merit was often measured by intricacy of design and
elaboration of workmanship, the Victorian house, large or small,
became a highly ornamental place, inside and out. Unfortunately
this passion for ornament did not achieve gaiety; it imposed fussi-
ness. A fresh generation of speculative builders adopted Ruskin's
advice about building Gothic porches and pointing windows.
The new suburbs that every city was thrusting into the countryside
displayed a mixture of ideas, drawn from German castles, French
chateaux and Italian Renaissance palaces. The simple, well-balanced
masses of classic architecture were replaced by intricate and broken
outlines. Roofs rose steeply and were variegated by gables, turrets
and dormer windows, surmounted by tile or cast iron crestings.
Ornamental tiling was used, also horizontal bands of different
coloured brickwork. English houses were no longer typical of
England. Before the early nineteenth century, new buildings in
town or country were regarded as improvements: in Victorian
times they were disfigurements.

The materials used were more varied than ever. Improved
transport made builders less dependent on local supplies; thus the
railway train and, later, the motor lorry, helped to destroy the
character of regional architecture. Materials were abundant;
there were few restrictions about the way they could be used. In
1850 the tax on bricks was repealed; the window tax was abolished
the following year.

Streets were seldom designed as complete architectural units:
Ruskin had said "do not think of unities of effect". So detached
and semi-detached houses, each planned without any relation to its
neighbours, became increasingly popular. When a street consisted
of a continuous row of houses, any orderly effect was defeated by
tiers of ill-shaped bay windows and by masses of meaningless,
super-imposed ornament. A few terraces of large houses were built
during the fifties; but they represented a dying fashion. Though
designed as complete architectural compositions, they were pom-
pous and lumbering, marred by debased ornament, and wholly
lacking in distinction.

In the countryside, the breakdown of all the old traditions of
regional building was beginning: the houses of the well-to-do
exhibited all the fussy elaboration of town houses, while cottages
were built with the same lack of invention, the same disregard for
human welfare, that had given the factory workers their grim
homes.

The middle-class householder was no longer satisfied by the simple
and convenient plan of the eighteenth-century house, with its few

---

[1] *Lectures on Architecture and Painting*, by John Ruskin. 1854.

large and well-proportioned rooms. His sense of importance demanded a house with as many rooms as possible, and as the value of land was constantly increasing, these houses had to be crowded into the same amount of space as that occupied by the older houses, thus reducing the size of rooms. So houses grew taller, four storeys or even higher. Great new blocks of dwellings towered up six, seven or eight storeys. Once again, as in the days of Piers Plowman, "High houses were regarded as a good investment for money."[1] In these tall houses and in the blocks of dwellings, which were called *tenements* when they accommodated what the Victorians called "the lower orders" and *flats* when they were inhabited by the middle and upper classes, the staircases lost their breadth; rooms were no longer a pleasant shape, they were just assembled without much relationship to each other, and all sorts of wasted spaces and odd corners appeared. The Victorian house builders dealt with any awkward-shaped space that occurred in a passage or on a landing, by putting a wooden framework in front of it, hanging a door, and calling it a cupboard. Those connecting passages were dark and rambling, and down in the basement, the service quarters were even darker. Upstairs, more light than ever was available.

The window tax was repealed in 1851, the Victorians liked lots of windows, and improvements in glass manufacture accommodated this liking. Sash windows could now be glazed with single large panes of plate glass, so that the rectangular window opening, while still retaining the proportion of the double square, was divided into two parts only. These large panes of excellent glass let in more light, but windows lost the neat appearance which the white-painted glazing bars had imparted to them in the Georgian age. To help in the diffusion of light, and also to secure additional privacy, these windows with their big plate glass panes were curtained with elaborate white lace. "It has been the fashion to laugh at the way the Victorians cluttered up their houses with all kinds of unnecessary frills, but the starched, white, lace curtain was a highly functional instrument for the diffusion of light. It has never been bettered for this purpose, because it provides absolute control over the diffusion of the light available, and, if drawn on a dull day, can give additional brightness to a room."[2]

The new, large-paned windows were often obstructed by elaborate developments of the window-box, so that the lower half of the sash opened upon a miniature green-house. "In the simplest form the window greenhouse was nothing more than an ornamental fern case placed upon the sill or hung from the window, but extensions of the idea gave the Victorian handyman a chance for those elaborations so dear to his heart. Complicated arrangements of plants and hanging baskets gave way, in households run by more

[1] See p. 46.   [2] *The Place of Glass in Building*, edited by John Gloag, p. 10.

MID-VICTORIAN INTERIOR

The furnishing of homes, large or small, became a process of accumulating a vast collection of objects, ornamental, useful and useless. Compare this congested room, overcrowded with clumsy furniture and overpowered with conflicting patterns, with the elegance and good proportion of the late eighteenth-century interior on page 125.

daring souls, to combined ornamental plant cases and *aquaria*, and in larger London villas to the inclusion of a fountain."[1]

In every room of the Victorian house there were ornamental patterns and decorative flourishes to arrest the eye; for householders had taken Ruskin's words to heart when he had written about "a general law, of singular importance in the present day, a law of simple common sense—not to decorate things belonging to purposes of active and occupied life. Wherever you can rest, there decorate; where rest is forbidden, so is beauty. You must not mix ornament with business, any more than you may mix play."[2] The home was the place for decoration, and builders, decorators and furnishers filled the homes of England with conflicting patterns, shapes and colours.

Though new and economical building materials were available, they were seldom allowed to display their real merits. In that age of sham they were used to ape traditional materials; elaborately figured wood was simulated by grained paintwork; great skill was lavished on producing the likeness of marble on plaster. Composition ornament could be pressed out by the mile, and all kinds of machine-made decoration was superimposed on every possible feature and article, for, like their Teutonic predecessors who conquered Roman Britain, the Victorians suffered from the "dread of blank space".[3] The description of the furnishing of a cottage ornée in *Handley Cross* suggests the pride that people took in rich and massive furnishing. When Captain Doleful wrote to Mr. Jorrocks about that desirable residence, Diana Lodge, he gave a list of the contents of the drawing room, which included ten chairs ". . . of massive imitation-rosewood, with beaded and railed backs and round knobs along the tops, and richly carved legs. In the centre is a beautiful round imitation-rosewood table on square lion-clawed brass castors, and the edge of the table is deeply inlaid with a broad circle of richly-carved, highly-polished brass." He mentioned "a fine flowered pattern" carpet, "richer than anything I can describe. . ."

In that rollicking story of Oxford, Cuthbert Bede's *Adventures of Mr. Verdant Green*, there is an account of the rooms of a wealthy undergraduate, who was supposed to be a man of taste. "The sitting room was large and lofty, and was panelled with oak throughout. At the further end was an elaborately carved book-case of walnut wood, filled with books gorgeously bound in every tint of morocco and vellum, with their backs richly tooled in gold." The walls, we are told, were thronged with water-colours; above them were groups of armour, and for the furniture, "there were couches of velvet, and lounging chairs of every variety and shape. There was a

---

[1] *Home: A Victorian Vignette*, by Robert Harling. "The Garden", pp. 52–53.
[2] *The Seven Lamps of Architecture*, by John Ruskin. Chap. IV, "The Lamp of Beauty", para. xix. [3] See quotation and footnote, Chap. II, p. 13.

Broadwood's grand piano-forte. . . . There were round tables and square tables, and writing tables; and there were side tables with statuettes and Swiss carvings, and old china, and gold apostle-spoons, and lava ware, and Etruscan vases, and a swarm of Spiers' elegant knick-knackeries. There were reading-stands of all sorts; Briarean-armed brazen ones, that fastened on to the chair you sat in —sloping ones to rest on the table before you, elaborately carved in open work, and an upright one of severe Gothic, like a lectern, where you were to stand and read without contracting your chest. Then there were all kinds of stands to hold books; sliding ones, expanding ones, portable ones, heavy fixture ones, plain mahogany ones, and oak ones made glorious by Margetts with the arms of Oxford and St. John's, carved and emblazoned on the ends."

Furniture was made in the darkest woods available—mahogany, rosewood, black walnut, bog oak—and over the surface of side-boards and cupboards, on overmantels and chimney-pieces, carving in the highest possible relief was used to depict flowers, fruit, animals and human figures. A sideboard shown at the Great Exhibition of 1851 was decorated with carved panels of scenes from Scott's *Kenilworth*. Such furniture was monumental in effect; most of it was well made, and nearly all of it was ill-proportioned and ungainly. Cheaper variations of it were produced in factories, and the machine was always used to imitate hand-made furniture. The term "machine-made" was used with contempt. Nobody thought of designing furniture which could be well made by machinery.

There were patterned carpets of violent colour; windows were draped with patterned damask, velvet or serge, trimmed with ball fringes, cords and tassels. Heavily patterned wallpapers were partly hidden by innumerable pictures in wide gilt frames. Heavily fringed tablecloths draped all the tables; fringed and bobbled runners drooped from the mantelshelves. Ornamental vases and knick-knacks filled every available space—ruby and gold Bohemian glass; turquoise, pink or apple green alabaster glass; garishly painted china; wax or wool flowers protected by large glass domes. Many of these ornaments had individual merit, but surrounded as they were by conflicting patterns, they merely added to the discords in a room. Papier maché furniture was very popular. This was lacquered black, inlaid with small chips of mother-of-pearl, and painted with bunches of flowers in realistic colours, and arabesques of gilt.

In the sitting and dining rooms, wallpapers were usually of heavy flock, deep red, green or blue, and patterned with greatly enlarged damask designs. In the passages and bedrooms, wallpapers had large floral designs—roses, lilies and violets being the favourites. Such flower patterns appeared again in the printed chintzes with which the windows were draped, but they seldom harmonised with the wallpaper. The carpets also displayed brightly-hued floral patterns.

The furniture, while not as massive as that in the downstairs rooms, was heavy enough. Huge wardrobes dominated the room. The dressing-table was draped with stiffly starched muslin petticoats, mounted over pink or blue silk, and the drapery continued over the mirror. In the middle of the century four-poster beds, or beds with a draped canopy were usual. These were followed by brass or iron bedsteads of repellent appearance. Towards the end of the century the old stuffy habit of drawing bed curtains at night had almost disappeared.

The warming pan, which previous generations of housewives had used for airing the sheets, was replaced by the stone hot water bottle. Every bedroom had a marble-topped wash-hand-stand with china basins and ewers. Flat shallow baths, or hip baths, were also part of bedroom equipment. They were of metal, painted on the outside to resemble grained wood, and were filled from large metal cans, painted and grained to match the baths.

In the fifties and sixties, bathrooms with a direct hot and cold water supply were rare. Surtees, describing a bedroom with "every imaginable luxury" at Hanby House in *Mr. Sponge's Sporting Tour*, includes "hip-baths, and foot-baths, a shower-bath, and hot and cold baths adjoining . . ." In the pages of *Punch*, the bathroom and the troubles of plumbing were occasionally subjects for the pencil of John Leech. A gentleman is depicted in one of the early oblong metal baths, framed in a wooden case, frantically pulling a bell cord amid clouds of steam, and shouting: "Hollo! Hi! Here! Somebody! I've turned on the hot water, and I can't turn it off again!" A swell with long, curly hair is advised by a short-haired old gentleman to use a conical oil-skin cap when taking a shower bath: a gentleman wearing such a cap is interrupted during his shower by the maid hammering on the bathroom door, and saying: "If you please, sir, here's the butcher, and missus says, what will you have for dinner to-day?" A grubby schoolboy disgusts his sisters by exclaiming: "Do you know, all the pipes are froze, and we shan't be able to have any of that horrid washing these cold mornings! Ain't it prime!" Under the title of "A trifle the matter with the kitchen boiler", another of Leech's drawings shows a top-hatted plumber and his mates removing the kitchen range and piling brickwork and rubble on the floor, while the master of the house looks on in despair. But before the end of the century, bathrooms were common though many people considered it was wrong and quite ridiculous to suggest that the houses of "the lower orders" should have such conveniences.

Bedrooms were still lit by oil lamps and candles, but in the town the principal living rooms were gas-lit. Cast iron and brass were fashioned into great branched gaseliers, suspended from the middle of the ceiling. The gas jets were protected from draught, at first by glass shades, made in the shape of an oil-lamp chimney; these gave place to glass globes which were sometimes plain, but often coloured rose pink or amber and decorated with painted sprays of flowers. Wall gas-brackets were of the same style as the pendant gaseliers.

Below stairs, the servants had to cope with immense and draughty basements, ill-lit and in need of constant scrubbing. All food had to be carried up a steep flight of stairs to the dining room, coals too had to be carried upstairs.

In the kitchen, the "patent kitchener" had become a vast cooking range on which the ample and elaborate Victorian meals could, with great waste of fuel, be efficiently cooked. In addition to a large table, the kitchen was generally furnished with an armchair for the cook and a few Windsor or rush-seated chairs for the other servants. A vast dresser occupied one wall. There were iron and copper pots and pans, and a variety of fancy decorated moulds for making puddings, aspics, mousses and shaped sweets.

During the second half of the century, a few artistic people rebelled against the stuffiness and elaboration of houses and furnishing. Of these rebels, by far the most influential was the poet and master-craftsman, William Morris. He had originally started life with the idea of becoming an architect; but he realised that architecture as it was practised in the middle years of the century, was something artificial, and that architects were too intent on waging "the battle of the styles" to be concerned with the welfare and practice of the crafts that served building. He regarded the architect as an intruder, a man who dictated from his drawing board how men should use their skill in woodwork and masonry, and with growing enthusiasm, he looked back to the Middle Ages, to the days when craftsmen were a band of brothers, working together; and building, unregulated by the Roman orders, was guided by the experience of the guilds and the laws made by their master-craftsmen. So he turned back to the past, and attempted to revive in a commercial machine age the handicrafts that had served an entirely different form of civilisation and a much smaller population. At Upton, in Kent, a house was built for him by an architect named Philip Webb. It was called the Red House, and it was the ancestor of a new romantic movement in domestic building. It had walls of warm red brick, a high-pitched red-tiled roof, and a cheerfully English air of having grown comfortably from the ground: it might have been built any time between 1480 and 1680 instead of in 1859. It has been copied and adapted with variations and additions, cheapened and vulgarised, by speculative builders for years; but its possibilities as a model were not recognised immediately, and Morris and his friends, who ignored the machine and who formed a company for the designing and making of furniture, wallpapers and fabrics, were regarded as cranks. One of the characters in *News from Nowhere*, which Morris described as "A Utopian romance", says: "England was once a country of clearings amongst the woods and wastes, with a few towns interspersed, which were fortresses for the feudal army, markets for the folk, gathering places for the craftsmen. It then became a country of huge and foul workshops, and fouler gambling-dens, surrounded by an ill-kept, poverty-stricken farm, pillaged by the masters of the workshops. It is now a garden, where nothing is wasted and nothing is spoilt, with the necessary dwellings, sheds, and workshops scattered up and down the country, all trim and neat and pretty. For, indeed, we should be too much ashamed of ourselves if we allowed the making of goods, even on a large scale, to carry with it the appearance, even, of desolation and misery."

Morris the poet, craftsman and socialist, wanted England to be like that; but the Arts and Crafts movement, which he started, was just another escape from realities, like the Gothic revival. In due time his work was to "Fill half the land with imitating fools . . ."

The influence of William Morris spread slowly, though it was some time before it became fashionable to be "artistic" and to dabble in the crafts.

By the eighties, although rooms were still overcrowded, heavily carved furniture was giving place to a lighter style, inlaid with patterns of marquetry. Harsh, bright colours became popular, for aniline dyes had been invented, and created a range of hues hitherto unobtainable with vegetable dyes. The colours themselves were good; but the vivid magentas, peacock blues and greens, and sharp pinks were used without discrimination.

These colours remained in vogue until what was called the "aesthetic movement" introduced a taste for more subdued tones. Rooms were then painted in drab olive greens and dull blue greys, and even—though this was considered daring—in white. Furniture was rather flimsy, and its form suggested a Japanese source, for it was made of bamboo. Japanese screens and various oriental odds and ends, blue and white china, peacock feathers and sunflowers, appeared in these fashionable rooms.

The majority of householders preferred comfort to fashion. They had plenty of it: deeply upholstered chairs, sofas and settees; hot and cold water; thick carpets and heavy curtains; high rooms and walls that were thick enough to be almost sound-proof. Some parts of the wall were padded, for the Victorian furnisher had invented the cosy corner. Not since the days of the Roman province of Britain had houses been so well-equipped, so warm and sanitary. Never before in the history of architecture had they been so badly planned, so wastefully built and so ugly. Privacy, comfort and novelty were honoured in houses large and small; commodity, firmness and delight had been forgotten.

A WILLIAM MORRIS ROOM.

CHAPTER XVI

THE TWENTIETH-CENTURY ENGLISHMAN'S CASTLE

VICTORIAN taste left the most conspicuous mark upon the cities, towns, villages and country houses of England, because in no previous period had so much building been done. The population of England and Wales had risen from just under fourteen millions in 1831 to over thirty-two-and-a-half millions in 1901. To accommodate this colossal increase, suburbs had overflowed from every city into the countryside, surrounding ancient villages and market towns. It seemed as though London must grow until it extended from Southend to Reading, and from Brighton to St. Albans. H. G. Wells, writing in 1902, said: "Great Towns before this century presented rounded contours and grew as a great puff-ball swells; the modern Great City looks like something that has burst an intolerable envelope and splashed."[1]

In every direction London had invaded rural areas; quiet villages like Putney, where Edward Gibbon was born in 1727 and which Dickens a century later still regarded as a remote and countrified place,[2] were now connected with London by continuous streets of houses. All this new development was Victorian; most of it was unplanned and dismally untidy. It had been carried out to meet the needs of the lower middle class, a thrifty and industrious section of the population. That great English journalist, Henry W. Nevinson, once described them and their ideal of home life in these words: "They are the shopkeepers, the clerks, the typists, the lower grades of the Civil Service, in short, the 'black-coated proletariat' who make up the majority of the 'bourgeoisie', and are therefore the objects of special scorn to Socialists and Communists. By thrift and application to a labour of monotonous routine, they have made for themselves nests in those innumerable little houses which stretch out for miles along all the suburban roads and by-passes of our great cities. Having risen to that point of comfort—to the peaceful enjoyment of a passage, a parlour, a back-room, a kitchen with a gas stove, electric light, two bedrooms upstairs, perhaps a bathroom, and certainly a separate and cleanly water-closet—they are very unwilling to sink to a lower standard of life, and down to that standard they perpetually fear to fall. A threat of losing their little savings or having their rents raised by taxation sends them

---

[1] *Anticipations*, by H. G. Wells. Sec. II, p. 45.   [2] See *David Copperfield*.

fluttering to the polls to vote Conservative. There is a sound of comfort and security in the very word. The Lower Middle Classes rather than the aristocracy have now become the bulwarks of the Constitution. Against revolution they would fight to the last, with their backs against the front doors."[1]

South of the river, London marched steadily into Kent and Surrey; northwards, it had reached Hampstead and Highgate. Here and there a few open spaces remained, such as Clapham and Wandsworth Commons. Old houses that had formerly marked the extent of some village like Battersea or Clapham, still survived with their mediaeval or eighteenth-century churches; but all about them the houses of the Victorian age displayed their fussy Gothic decoration, their clumsy bay windows of sand-coloured Bath stone, their cheap yellow, hard red or dusty grey bricks, set in dark mortar, their purple slate roofs, and their spiky cast-iron front railings and gates. On the face of those houses drain pipes were fixed, to carry water from gutters and bathrooms; they were never made part of the design; like chimney-pots, they seemed to be awkward afterthoughts. There were plainer houses with painted stucco fronts, and a few ill-placed classical ornaments and features, the last traces of John Nash's influence. This type is described and illustrated in that entertaining account of lower middle class life in the 'nineties, *The Diary of a Nobody*, by George and Weedon Grossmith. Charles Pooter, who kept the *Diary*, described his semi-detached home, "The Laurels", Brickfield Terrace, Holloway, as "a nice six-roomed residence, not counting basement, with a front breakfast-parlour. We have a little front garden; and there is a flight of ten steps up to the front door, which, by-the-by, we keep locked with the chain up . . . our . . . intimate friends always coming to the little side entrance, which saves the servant the trouble of going up to the front door, thereby taking her from her work. We have a nice little back garden which runs down to the railway."

That last sentence shows the sort of muddle unplanned development by speculative builders had created; but it seemed natural to the Victorians that the garden of a house should run down to a noisy railway as it had seemed natural to the highly civilised Georgians that a garden should be bordered by some placid stream. Gas-works and warehouses, smoke-producing workshops and busy railway goods yards were intermingled with schools, hospitals and streets of houses over vast areas. The "Removal of such *Trades*, as are manifest *Nuisances* to the City" which John Evelyn had advocated in 1661, had never been regarded as practical; but apart from obeying the recommendations of a Royal Commission, which in 1846 had determined "that all railways within a certain radius were to be underground," the various authorities and great landowners,

[1] *Ourselves, an Essay on the National Character*, by Henry W. Nevinson, pp. 33–34.

whose laws, rights and whims governed the metropolis, allowed London to grow anyhow and anywhere.[1]

There were exceptions among the nineteenth-century speculative builders who developed London's suburbs; some had inherited a respect for spacious and civilised planning. For example, when Thomas Cubitt had developed Clapham Park south-west of Clapham Common, "he began constructing four miles of wide roadway and making a nursery of thousands of trees, for transplantation as the houses on the estate were ready to receive them."[2] But in every way Thomas Cubitt was exceptional. "He published one of of the first plans for the general drainage of London, urging that the city's sewage should be carried well down the Thames before being allowed to mix with the river water. In advance of the act which dealt with smoke abatement, he fitted his own works at Thames Bank with appliances which successfully prevented the escape of smoke. He was a warm advocate for the provision of public parks, while the necessary land could still be bought cheaply. He had leased from the Marquess of Westminster a tract of swampy ground partly cultivated by cabbage and asparagus growers; and he framed a scheme, which he submitted to the Metropolitan Improvement Commissioners, for making there a park for the people. The Government accepted the scheme, and when later on Disraeli, as Chancellor of the Exchequer, opposed it, and the project was in jeopardy, Thomas Cubitt helped to secure its passage by offering to buy from the Government, for what they had cost, both the land and the bridge concerned."[3]

In 1898 a book had been published entitled *To-morrow*. The author was Ebenezer Howard, and he described a new type of town, which was called a "garden city". It was re-issued in 1902 under the title of *Garden Cities of To-morrow*. Howard's proposal for a garden city has been summarised by Mr. C. B. Purdom as follows: "An estate of 6000 acres was to be bought at a cost of £40 an acre, or £240,000. The estate was to be held in trust, 'first, as a security for the debenture-holders, and, secondly, in trust for the people of Garden City'. A town was to be built near the centre of the estate to occupy about 1000 acres. Six boulevards were to divide the town into six equal parts. In the centre was to be a park in which were placed the public buildings, and around the park a great arcade containing shops, etc. The population of the town was to be 30,000. The building plots were to be of an average size of 20 by 130 feet. There were to be common gardens and co-operative kitchens. On the outer ring of the town there were to be factories, warehouses, etc., fronting on a circular railway. The agricultural estate of 5000 acres was to be properly developed for agricultural

[1] *London: The Unique City*, by Steen Eiler Rasmussen. Chap. VII, p. 135.
[2] *Man and Boy*, by Sir Stephen Tallents. Sec. II, p. 33.   [3] *Ibid.*, Sec. II, p. 34.

purposes as part of the scheme, and the population of this belt was taken at 2000."[1]

The idea of the garden city appealed not only to the middle classes, but to many speculative builders, who applied the name to almost any housing scheme where a few original trees survived and the front and back gardens were a little larger than usual. This spacious form of suburban development increased the demand for detached and semi-detached houses; it made the Victorian streets and terraces seem cramped and out-of-date, and it encouraged hundreds of builders to imitate the character of the Red House that Philip Webb had built for William Morris. Thus a new form of romantic architecture arose, less solid than the early Victorian romantic style, but satisfying the householder's desire for picturesque and cosy surroundings. Suburban villas began to look like enlarged cottages. By comparison with a Victorian house, their rooms were smaller and the ceilings much lower. The sash window with its large plate glass panes was replaced by the casement with leaded lights, and in the front door a panel of stained glass, or half a dozen bullions or bull's eyes framed in wood or lead, admitted a little dim light to the hall. These bullions were the scars or lumps that occurred in the old process of making glass, and in the seventeenth and eighteenth centuries cottagers were glad enough to have them in their windows, because there was nothing better available: for a very different reason the Edwardian householder who lived in an artistic "garden" suburb, was glad to accept such an imperfect article. The Victorians had often used cheap materials and mechanical methods to imitate costly and elaborate finishes; the Edwardians went to any amount of trouble to imitate materials that, in former ages, had been considered crude and cheap. They were delighted by finishes and textures that skill and invention had long rendered obsolete. There was a fashion for "hand-made" things, and metalwork was often speckled with hammer marks—put on by machinery —to suggest that it was the work of a toiling craftsman. This was one result of the arts and crafts movement that William Morris had started; another was the awakening of a lively interest in old houses and old furniture. In practice, Morris's ideas were widely misrepresented; for example, the small houses produced by speculative builders were furnished with cheap imitations of features that had arisen naturally in the course of Morris's attempt to restore old methods of building. Stained slats of wood were nailed on to the face of brickwork to imitate the timber-framing of the late fifteenth and sixteenth centuries: every little villa had to look like a Tudor manor in miniature, with a gable crowning its projecting bay window.

[1] *Town Theory and Practice*, edited by C. B. Purdom. Introductory Chapter, pp. 19–20.

Fashionable folk filled their houses with old furniture, and began to study "period" styles. The antique dealers began to thrive. People no longer wanted the newest and latest designs; they wanted the very oldest relics. The collecting of antique furniture, or the buying of machine-produced furniture that imitated antique forms, seemed to satisfy every section of the public. The appearance of such furniture certainly provided a link with "the good old times", and the early twentieth-century English, home became strangely dependent upon the past for its ideas. Never before in the history of house building had so many materials and mechanical processes been available; but builders and manufacturers seemed afraid to use them, except for purposes of imitation. Perhaps the last "original" style in furnishing and decoration had something to do with this reluctance to experiment with new forms.

At the end of the nineteenth century a strange and restless fashion known as "New Art", had spread over the Continent, at last reaching England where for a few years it was regarded as really "modern". In 1897 "Van de Velde was startling Europe with his celebrated *art-nouveau* Rest-Room at the Dresden Art Exhibition";[1] but England was even more startled by this new fashion. It was characterised by wriggling curves and arabesques; by florid, writhing plant forms, leaves and stems that wound over chairs, tables, wall-paper, mantel-pieces and overmantels. Where the Elizabethan interior had reflected the splendour of the tropical forest, the Edwardian "New Art" interior suggested the fevered complexity of the mangrove swamp. Every surface was packed with ornament: there were panels in contrasting woods, carved scrolls and loops, painted and stained patterns, and inlays of such materials as enamel, mother-of-pearl, and polished copper. Textiles were woven in florid patterns or stencilled on plain grounds. Vases, lamps, and household ornaments of glass and china all followed the same forms. There was no peace for the eye; none of the solid, dull and comparatively restful comfort of Victorian furnishing and interior decoration. No wonder people turned with a sense of relief from this worrying and strenuous fashion to the pleasant and exciting task of collecting antique furniture, genuine or faked. Everybody began to borrow ideas from the past. A large town or country house in the opening decades of the century might have a late Tudor dining room, an Adam drawing room, a Regency morning room, Queen Anne, early Georgian and late Stuart bedrooms; with electric light everywhere, the glass bulbs sprouting from white porcelain tubes, in imitation of candles, so the form of "period" chandeliers and wall brackets would not be marred. A little steam heating would supplement the coal fires; telephone instruments would be tactfully

[1] *Scenario for a Human Drama*, by P. Morton Shand. *The Architectural Review*, January 1935, p. 26.

concealed in damask-covered dome-topped cases or in adapted eighteenth-century mahogany knife-boxes; and in the bathrooms, plumbing of super-Roman luxury would be found. Decorators and furnishers were determined to conceal all evidence of the machine age. Even electric bells were operated by tasselled bell cords, hung from the frieze.

Gas was used not only for lighting, but for cooking and water heating. The incandescent mantle had improved the power and purity of gas lighting, and the dully glowing carbon bulbs at first used for electric light compared badly with the gas mantle. But the brilliant and powerful metallic filament bulb replaced the carbon, and gas gradually lost its popularity for lighting, though it remained the principal form of power for cooking and supplementary heating. The gas stove, convenient, compact and easily managed, made kitchens everywhere cleaner and more agreeable; fuel-burning cooking stoves were also greatly improved in design. Kitchens were smaller, for they no longer accommodated a huge cooking range, and as new houses seldom had basements, they received the benefit of daylight and fresh air.

Although most of the house building was done by speculative builders, several talented architects were at work in the Edwardian period. They built individual houses, generally in the country, and in their early designs the influence of that famous model, the Red House, was apparent. C. F. A. Voysey and Sir Edwin Lutyens are the two outstanding names. Voysey's houses had a clean simplicity of form; they were ample and homely, and they made the most appropriate use of materials; within, they had an air of orderly spaciousness. They were a development of the English tradition of domestic building, which had lasted until the seventeenth century; and, except for some of the materials used, they might, like the Red House, have been built during the two centuries between 1480 and 1680. (They provided fresh material for imitation by the speculative builder.) Sir Edwin Lutyens, the last great English architect to design in the Renaissance tradition, had in the 'nineties, built some large country houses; and they also had close kinship with sixteenth- and seventeenth-century country houses of the type that were modestly unconcerned with fashion. But early in the twentieth century, Sir Edwin gave to the classic style a new injection of genius in a house called Heathcote, in Yorkshire. It had the symmetry, the harmonious proportions and the easy dignity of great architecture. Heathcote and many of his later buildings revealed that an English architect was in practice, whose work could be ranked with the best that was produced in the eighteenth century.

Some furniture designers of great distinction were at this time making beautiful and very costly things by hand in various country

COUNTRY HOUSE OF THE TYPE DESIGNED 1900-1910.

retreats; of these Ernest Gimson and Sidney Barnsley produced work that was comparable with that of the great Georgian cabinet-makers. They were interpreting the ideas of William Morris, by reviving sound craftsmanship, and they continued the sturdy English traditions of mid-seventeenth-century furniture-making. They never imitated older models; their furniture was original in design, unmistakably and refreshingly English in character. The work of another designer, Sir Ambrose Heal, had great influence on contemporary taste, and his furniture, which was simple and well proportioned and unmarred by dark staining and polishing, was within the reach of ordinary people. Apart from the exclusive and enormously expensive work of artist-craftsmen like Gimson, the only genuine twentieth-century furniture before 1914 was Heal's. After the first world war, other designers organised the production of modern furniture; and of these Gordon Russell was the most outstanding. All these master-designers of furniture used the colour and figure of wood to the best advantage; they allowed clean surfaces of English oak and English walnut to provide the decorative interest; they never "applied" mouldings; they seldom used carving, but they were skilful in their use of inlays. Such furniture enabled people to see what fine woods really looked like; for generations the rich hues and markings of oak, walnut and mahogany, had been concealed by deep-toned, high polishes; and since the start of the craze for collecting antiques, everything had to look like "old oak". It was many years before the furniture manufacturing trade made any attempt to follow such original and adventurous leadership.

There was a revival of classic architecture at the close of the Edwardian period: rather heavy-handed variations of Queen Anne and early Georgian houses were built, but the straightforward simplicity of the original models was marred by the excessive elaboration of such features as porches and chimney stacks. Many architects tried their hand at improving the Roman orders: they overloaded capitals with additional carving that hung down in swags and festoons over the columns; they belted the columns with square blocks of stone; they stuck little obelisks of stone here, there and everywhere; they packed pediments, cornices and keystones with ornamentation. The ideas of Norman Shaw, whose works included Scotland Yard and the Piccadilly Hotel in London, had encouraged this new interest in classic design. But Shaw was an architect of commanding ability: he could take liberties with ancient forms: his imitators only too often achieved the confused and restless results that had marred Elizabethan architecture.

In the course of this revival of classic forms, the Georgian sash window with its glazing bars and small rectangular panes, was restored to favour. In due time, the speculative builders began to copy these houses, often using sash windows for "Tudor" and other picturesque villas in suburban development.

In 1903 the first garden city was built at Letchworth in Hertfordshire. "First Garden City Limited was incorporated under the Companies Acts, with an authorised capital of £300,000 to purchase an estate of 3818 acres (since increased to 4500 acres), and to establish thereon a town, with industries, with a population of 30,000 in accordance with the scheme set out by Mr. Howard in his book. The dividends on the share capital were limited to 5 per cent and the balance of the profits of the Company were to go to the community."[1]

The Hampstead Garden Suburb was also planned and largely built before the 1914–18 war, and in 1919 Welwyn Garden City was laid out. The war interrupted domestic building, and after it there was a great shortage of houses. The population of England and Wales had increased from 32,527,843 in 1901, to 37,886,699 in 1921; thousands of men in the services who had married during the war wanted homes, and they were promised "homes fit for heroes to live in". Many housing estates were planned for local authorities by architects, and simple and agreeable houses were built, though not nearly enough of them to satisfy the demand. Most of these estates were well laid out; old trees were kept, new trees planted; and they acquired an air of spaciousness and order. Great new roads were planned to carry the vastly increased motor traffic; and ribbon development, which in Victorian times had followed railways out of every city and had bordered them with thousands of back gardens, now followed the new traffic roads and bordered them with the front gardens of brick-built, imitation half-timbered suburban villas. The Victorian householders were protected from the trains that shook their homes, day and night: there were fences and penalties to prevent them from crossing the tracks except by proper bridges. Nothing protected householders from the motor traffic that roared along the new roads, and which grew denser and faster year after year.

This ribbon development was the work of speculative builders; all over the country fresh areas were labelled as "ripe for development", trees were felled, fine old buildings demolished, and acre after acre of cheap, jerry-built and badly planned villas were erected. Once more London surged outwards into the country. New residential areas were opened up by extensions of the Tube railways and 'bus routes, and by the electrification of new sections of the main line railways.

Some speculative housing schemes were well planned and care was taken to preserve open spaces and trees. Local authorities had legal powers to plan both town and country, but they were not

[1] *Town Theory and Practice*, edited by C. B. Purdom. Introductory Chapter, pp. 24–25.

During the nineteen-twenties many individual houses and large housing schemes were built in the Georgian manner. Such buildings did not represent slavish copying: they made use of methods and features that had been tested and found satisfactory during the greatest period of English domestic architecture.

generally used. The country had not recovered from the Victorian period, when respect for order and tidiness had vanished, together with good design in architecture. Early in the nineteenth century some people had accepted jerry-building because it looked genteel: a hundred years later it was accepted because it looked cosy and picturesque. Thousands of jerry-built villas were filled with machine-made imitations of Jacobean and Georgian furniture; the twentieth-century Englishman's castle had become a museum of flimsy parodies of things used generations earlier. Even radio sets were, at first, dolled-up to look like old oak cupboards.

Houses built by architects displayed the graces of the eighteenth century, with many agreeable variations, and a revival of taste for Georgian architecture exerted a marked influence on building generally. Some of the big municipal housing schemes, like that at Prescot near Liverpool, might have been designed and built a hundred and fifty years earlier; and many of the slum-clearance schemes, in which England led the world, reproduced the characteristic features of the Georgian period.

Never before had there been so many varied materials for building and so many appliances that saved labour, increased comfort, and furnished entertainment. Not even in the Victorian period had there been so much confusion of thought about the way to use building materials. A young, progressive generation of architects turned impatiently from this confusion. They practised what began to be called "the modern movement", and they were unfortunately attracted by a glib, foreign phrase: "The house is a machine for living in." The man who wrote that, M. Le Corbusier, also wrote: "Men—intelligent, cold and calm—are needed to build the house and to lay out the town."[1] Many of the architects who built "modern" houses took that to heart, and their designs were strictly functional: like John Pomfret, they decided that when they equipped a house:

> "It should, within, no other Things contain
> But what were Useful, Necessary, Plain . . ."

In the process of being "intelligent, cold and calm", they were inclined to forget that ornament is an ancient human need and that an Englishman likes privacy and comfort. Many of the houses designed by those earnest and occasionally talented architects, were based on what they thought people *ought* to want instead of what most people wanted. (The speculative builders knew far more about human nature.) The "modernist" architects fell in love with the forms that reinforced concrete made possible: they liked flat roofs and long, horizontal windows stretching across the front of a building, and by indulging their taste for such things they deprived houses of useful lofts and box-rooms under the roof, while the long windows which looked so modish from the outside, made the rooms behind them rather bleak and comfortless. "Large expanses of glass in a room increase the cost of heating in winter, and demand a heavy outlay on fabrics for covering the transparent wall at night. The need for privacy, the site of the house, or flat, and the character of the climate in these islands should determine the area of transparency in any room. No room should be denied abundant daylight, but 'a wall of glass' may bring a surfeit, which compels the occupants to mask the window, and reduce its size to bearable proportions."[2]

The modern movement, which was at first hailed as a new way of thinking that would bring about a new way of life, exercised some influence on English house building in the nineteen-thirties; but its forms were often based on the extraordinary belief that England is a land of hot and almost continuous sunshine. On a cold, damp November or February day, those ultra-modern houses looked and indeed were, anything but comfortable. After a few years of exposure to the English climate, they looked shoddy and woebegone, and were streaked with dirty smears where rain had dribbled down the walls, for they were unprotected by cornice or coping, and were sliced off at the top, as if they had been cut from sheets of cardboard. Many of these "machines for living in" had "functional" furniture of metal and fabrics; chromium-plated tubular steel providing frames for chairs and tables.

[1] *Towards a New Architecture*, by Le Corbusier, translated from the thirteenth French edition, by Frederick Etchells, p. 127.
[2] *The Place of Glass in Building*, edited by John Gloag, p. 9.

1942 HOUSING SCHEME FOR WAR-WORKERS, DESIGNED BY G. A. JELLICOE, F.R.I.B.A.

The modern movement was only represented by a tiny proportion of the houses built in the the ten years before the second world war; but in that time, the speculative builders ran up a few trial houses with flat roofs and wide windows, built of white-washed brick in imitation of concrete. If they didn't sell at first, it was easy enough to clap a pitched roof on top to make the shape more familiar.

The modern movement, which began in England with Voysey's clear-sighted use of the most appropriate materials for creating large, uncomplicated spaces for living, grew slowly in Europe and the United States during the first quarter of the century. It has led to an immense amount of writing and talking: it is, perhaps, the reflection of the machine age in terms of architecture: it may well be the crude beginnings of a new style, as potent and universal as the classic architecture of Greece and Rome and the Gothic forms that were perfected during the Middle Ages. So far no great English architect has understood and controlled and interpreted its possibilities, as Inigo Jones mastered and interpreted the Italianate architecture of the Renaissance. The modern movement does not yet speak English. It has so far been regarded, though not acknowledged, as a fashion. Those who have practised it, have sometimes forgotten that they are architects and have become social reformers, intent on telling their fellow-countrymen how they should live, instead of providing them with the best background for living in their own way.

The Englishman's way of living is now seven centuries deep. His house is still his castle, whether it is large or small, in town, country, surburb or garden city. It is certainly not "a machine for living in": it is something more human and civilised and comfortable —it is a home. Despite a hundred years of confusion and vulgarity in taste and lack of education and judgment in design, the English home still shows the Englishman's mastery of the art of living a private life.

APPENDIX

SOME NOTES ON BOOKS TO READ

No study of English house building is possible without interest being aroused in the much larger subject of architecture. In the interval between the two world wars, many excellent and readable books were written on architecture and design. Those who wish to amplify the information contained in the sixteen chapters of this book, may read with profit some of the volumes suggested in the following list: they are neither dry nor highly technical.

ON ARCHITECTURE AND BUILDING

ABERCROMBIE, PATRICK.

The Book of the Modern House. Hodder & Stoughton Ltd., 1939. Professor Abercrombie has edited a survey of contemporary domestic architecture, in town and country.

BARMAN, CHRISTIAN.

Architecture. Ernest Benn, Ltd., 1928. A short, compact history of architecture.

BETJEMAN, JOHN.

Ghastly Good Taste. Chapman & Hall, Ltd., 1933. Described by the the author as "a depressing story of the rise and fall of English Architecture".

BOUMPHREY, GEOFFREY.

Your House and Mine. Allen & Unwin, Ltd., 1935. A survey of the effect of social influences on house design.

BRADDALL, D'ARCY.

How to Look at Buildings. Methuen, 1930. A practical guide to architectural character, instructive and aptly illustrated.

BRAUN, HUGH.

The Story of the English House. Batsford, Ltd., 1940. An admirably illustrated and well told history of English house building.

BYRON, ROBERT.

The Appreciation of Architecture. Wishart & Co., 1932. An essay on the principles of composition and design.

CLARK, SIR KENNETH.

The Gothic Revival. Constable & Co., 1928. A most illuminating history of the growth and influence of the taste for Gothic architecture in the nineteenth century.

EDWARDS, A. TRYSTAN.
Architectural Style. Faber, 1926. An illustrated examination of the principles of design and their relation to good taste in architecture.

GIBBERD, FREDERICK.
The Architecture of England from Norman Times to the Present Day. Architectural Press, 1938. A pictorial history of English architecture.

GLOAG, JOHN.
Men and Buildings. Country Life, Ltd., 1933. A short historical account of the influences that have helped to form the character of English architecture.

LEATHART, JULIAN.
Style in Architecture. THOMAS NELSON & SONS, LTD., 1940. A history of the growth and nature of style in architecture.

MCGRATH, RAYMOND.
Twentieth Century Houses. Faber & Faber, 1933. This book, written in basic English, reviews modern architecture in Britain, Europe and the United States. It has excellent illustrations.

PEVSNER, NIKOLAUS.
An Outline of European Architecture. Pelican Books, 1942. An illustrated, condensed history of architecture from the sixth century to the twentieth.

PHILLIPPS, LISLE MARCH.
The Works of Man. Duckworth. Second edition, 1914. Describes how national character leaves its imprint on art and architecture.

QUENNELL, MARJORIE AND C. H. B.
A History of Everyday Things in England. Batsford Ltd., 1918. An illustrated and pleasantly discursive account of everything connected with design for living—houses, toys, castles, clothes, armour, ships, coaches and food—from 1066 to 1799.

RICHARDS, J. M.
An Introduction to Modern Architecture. Penguin Books, 1940. It describes the growth and development of ideas that modern architecture seeks to express.

RICHARDS, J. M.
A Miniature History of the English House. Architectural Press, 1938. A brief history, largely pictorial.

RICHARDSON, A. E., and CORFIATO, HECTOR O.
The Art of Architecture. The English Universities' Press, Ltd., 1938. A comprehensive and copiously illustrated history of architectural composition.

ROBERTSON, HOWARD.
Architecture Explained. Ernest Benn, Ltd., 1927. A history of architecture from the earliest times, with chapters on architectural design.

ROYAL INSTITUTE OF BRITISH ARCHITECTS.
Rebuilding Britain. Lund Humphries, 1943. This glances at the future: it describes the work of the Reconstruction Committee of the R.I.B.A., and illustrates a number of possibilities.

WILLIAMS-ELLIS, C. and A.
The Pleasures of Architecture. Jonathan Cape, Ltd. Life and Letters Series, 1924. An informative and diverting book.

WILLIAMS-ELLIS, CLOUGH, and SUMMERSON, JOHN.
Architecture Here and Now. Thomas Nelson & Sons, Ltd., 1934. A fully illustrated account of contemporary architecture.

YORKE, F. R. S. AND PENN, COLIN.
A Key to Modern Architecture. Blackie, 1939. An explanation of some of the principles of modern architecture.

BOOKS REFERRED TO IN THE TEXT

Note.—Where references to any work occur in more than one chapter, an asterisk appears beside the name of the book.

There are certain standard works which have been referred to in the course of writing this book, notably: *A History of Architecture on the Comparative Method,* by SIR BANISTER FLETCHER; *A History of the English House,* by NATHANIEL LLOYD; *Theory and Elements of Architecture,* by ROBERT ATKINSON and HOPE BAGENAL.

CHAPTER I

Great Britain: Essays in Regional Geography, by twenty-six authors. Edited by Sir E. J. Russell, D.Sc., F.R.S., Cambridge University Press, 1928.

A Pocket Book of British Trees, by E. H. B. BOULTON, M.A. A. & C. Black, Ltd., 1937.

Theory and Elements of Architecture, by ROBERT ATKINSON, F.R.I.B.A., and HOPE BAGENAL, A.R.I.B.A. Ernest Benn, Ltd., 1926.

The Architecture of Marcus Vitruvius Pollio, translated by JOSEPH GWILT. Priestley & Weale, 1826.

Architecture Explained, by HOWARD ROBERTSON, F.R.I.B.A. Ernest Benn, Ltd., 1927.

CHAPTER II

The Earlier Inhabitants of London, by F. G. PARSONS, F.R.C.S., F.S.A. Cecil Palmer, 1927.

Along the Roman Roads, by GEOFFREY BOUMPHREY. George Allen & Unwin, Ltd., 1935.

Romano-British Buildings and Earthworks, by JOHN WARD, F.S.A. Methuen & Co., 1911.

Londinium, Architecture and the Crafts, by W. R. LETHABY. Duckworth & Co., 1923.

Reading Museum Guide to the Silchester Collection, by MILL STEPHENSON. Seventh edition, Poynder & Son, Reading, 1927.

*Anglo-Saxon Art, by T. D. KENDRICK, F.S.A. Methuen & Co., 1938.

Victoria County History, Hampshire and the Isle of Wight, Romano-British section by F. HAVERFIELD. Vol. I. Constable.

The Itinerary through Wales, by GIRALDUS CAMBRENSIS. Everyman Library.

Dog and Duck, by ARTHUR MACHEN. Travellers' Library, Jonathan Cape, 1926.

CHAPTER III

Bede's Ecclesiastical History. Everyman Library.

Heimskringla: the Olaf Sagas, by SNORRE STURLASON. Everyman Library.

Roman Britain and the English Settlements, by R. G. COLLINGWOOD and J. N. L. MYRES. Oxford, Clarendon Press, 1936.

*A History of English Art in the Middle Ages, by C. ELFRIDA SAUNDERS. Oxford Clarendon Press, 1932.

The Development of English Building Construction, by C. F. INNOCENT, A.R.I.B.A. Cambridge University Press, 1916.

*The Evolution of the English House, by S. O. ADDY. George Allen & Unwin, Ltd. Revised edition, 1935.

*A History of the English House, by NATHANIEL LLOYD. Architectural Press, 1931.

London before the Conquest, by W. R. LETHABY. Macmillan & Co., Ltd., 1902.

CHAPTER IV

The Architect's Journal, Vol. 85, No. 2198. March 4, 1937. "Sanitation: an historical survey", by H. A. J. LAMB, A.R.I.B.A.

*The Official Architect, Vol. 4, No. 4, April 1941. "Sanitation through the Ages", by DESMOND EYLES.

Mediaeval England, 1066–1350, by MARY BATESON. Fisher Unwin, 1903.

*A History of Domestic Manners and Sentiments in England during the Middle Ages, by THOMAS WRIGHT, M.A., F.S.A. Chapman & Hall, 1862.

Tattershall Castle, Lincolnshire: a Historical and Descriptive Survey, by the late LORD CURZON and H. AVERY TIPPING. Jonathan Cape, 1929.

The Mediaeval Village, by G. G. COULTON. Cambridge University Press. 1925.

Life on the English Manor, 1150–1400, by H. S. BENNETT, M.A. Cambridge University Press, 1937.

Survey of London, by JOHN STOWE. Everyman Library.

CHAPTER V

Social Life in the Days of Piers Plowman, by D. CHADWICK. Cambridge University Press, 1922.

The Master of Game, by EDWARD, SECOND DUKE OF YORK. Edited by W. A. and F. BAILLIE-GROHMAN. Chatto & Windus, 1909.

CHAPTER VI

Harrison's Description of England, edited by Frederick T. Furnivall from the first two editions of Holinshed's Chronicle, 1577–1587. The New Shakespeare Society, 1877–1878.

CHAPTER VII

The English Voyages of the Sixteenth Century, by SIR WALTER RALEIGH. James MacLehose & Sons, Glasgow. 1906.

The Artisan in Elizabethan Literature, by CHARLES W. CAMP. Columbia University Press, New York, 1924.

England as seen by Foreigners in the Days of Elizabeth and James I, by WILLIAM BRENCHLEY RYE. John Russell Smith, London, 1865.

CHAPTER VIII

Some Architectural Works of Inigo Jones, by H. INIGO TRIGGS and HENRY TANNER, JN. Batsford, 1901.

Glass in Architecture and Decoration, by RAYMOND McGRATH and A. C. FROST. The Architectural Press, 1937.

The Englishman's Food, A History of Five Centuries of English Diet, by J. C. DRUMMOND and ANNE WILBRAHAM. Jonathan Cape, 1939.

CHAPTER IX

Evelyn's Diary.

CHAPTER X

Inigo Jones, by STANLEY C. RAMSEY. Ernest Benn, Ltd., 1924.

Fumifugium, or the Inconvenience of the Aer and the Smoake of London Dissi-pated, by JOHN EVELYN. Reprint published by National Smoke Abatement Society, 1933.

Pepys' Diary.

The England of Charles II, by ARTHUR BRYANT. Longmans, 1934.

London: The Unique City, by STEEN EILER RASMUSSEN. Jonathan Cape, 1934.

Cottage Economy, by WILLIAM COBBETT. Stereotype edition, C. Clement, 1822.

CHAPTER XI

Masterpieces of English Furniture and Clocks, by R. W. SYMONDS. Batsford, 1940.

A Critical Review of the Public Buildings, Statues and Ornaments, in, and about, London and Westminster, ANON. Printed by C. Ackers in St. John's Street, for J. Wilford behind the chapter house in St. Paul's Churchyard, and J. Clarke at the Golden Ball in Duck Lane, 1734.

CHAPTER XII

Practical Decoration of Furniture, by H. P. SHAPLAND. Ernest Benn, Ltd., 1927.

A History of Architecture on the Comparative Method, by SIR BANISTER FLETCHER. Batsford (Eighth edition), 1929.

Sir John Vanbrugh, by CHRISTIAN BARMAN. Ernest Benn, Ltd., 1924.

Social Life in the Reign of Queen Anne, by JOHN ASHTON. Chatto & Windus, 1883.

CHAPTER XIII

The European Magazine, November, 1798.

English Men and Manners in the Eighteenth Century, by A. S. TURBERVILLE. Oxford University Press, 1926.

Architectural Design and Construction, Vol. I, No. 1, November, 1930.

London and its Environs Described. Printed for R. and J. Dodsley, Pall-Mall, 1761.

The Smaller English House of the Later Renaissance, 1660–1830, by A. E. RICHARDSON and H. DONALDSON EBERLEIN. Batsford, 1925.

Horace Walpole, by R. W. KETTON-CREMER. Duckworth & Co., 1940.

A Catalogue of the Wedgwood Museum, Etruria, by FREDERICK RATHBONE. Josiah Wedgwood and Sons, Ltd., Stoke-on-Trent, 1909.

CHAPTER XIV

Timber Houses, edited by E. H. B. Boulton. Country Life, Limited, 1937.

The Quarterly Review, XXXIV. 1826.

John Nash, by JOHN SUMMERSON. George Allen & Unwin, Ltd., 1935.

The New Monthly Magazine, 1825.

Metropolitan Improvements, by THOMAS H. SHEPARD. Published by Jones & Co., Temple of the Muses, Finsbury Square, London, April 11, 1829.

CHAPTER XV

Lectures on Architecture and Painting, by JOHN RUSKIN. Universal Edition: Routledge.

*The Place of Glass in Building, edited by John Gloag. George Allen & Unwin, Ltd., 1943.

Home: A Victorian Vignette, by ROBERT HARLING. Constable, 1938.

The Seven Lamps of Architecture, by JOHN RUSKIN. Universal Edition: Routledge.

CHAPTER XVI

Anticipations, by H. G. WELLS. Chapman & Hall, 1902.

Ourselves, an Essay on the National Character, by HENRY W. NEVINSON. British Broadcasting Corporation, 1933.

Man and Boy, by SIR STEPHEN TALLENTS. Faber & Faber, 1943.

Town Theory and Practice, edited by C. B. Purdom. Benn Brothers, Ltd., 1921.

The Architectural Review, January 1935.

Towards a New Architecture, by LE CORBUSIER. Translated from the thirteenth French edition, with an introduction by Frederick Etchells. John Rodker, 1927.

THE FOLLOWING WORKS WERE CONSULTED IN CONNECTION WITH THE ILLUSTRATIONS

The History of the English House, by NATHANIEL LLOYD. Architectural Press, 1931.

A History of Architecture in England (in two volumes), by WALTER H. GODFREY. Batsford, 1931.

A History of Architecture, by G. FISKE KIMBALL and G. H. EDGELL. Batsford, 1917.

William Morris, Designer, by GERALD H. CROW. "The Studio" Winter Number, 1934.

The Illustrated London News, April, 1926.

Romano-British Buildings and Earthworks, by JOHN WARD, F.S.A. Methuen & Co., 1911.

Old England, a Pictorial Museum, by CHARLES KNIGHT. James Sangster, 1850.

The Art Journal (Thomas Wright's History of Domestic Manners).

Britain's Story told in Pictures, by C. W. NAIRNE. Sankey Hudson.

Everyday Life in Roman Britain, by MARJORIE and C. H. B. QUENNELL. Batsford, 1924.

The Arts of the Middle Ages, by PAUL LACROIX. J. & S. Virtue, 1870.

The Mansions of England in the Olden Time, by JOSEPH NASH. "The Studio" Winter Number, 1905-06.

The Smaller English House of the Later Renaissance, 1660-1830, by A. E. RICHARDSON and H. DONALDSON EBERLEIN. Batsford, 1925.

London Cameos, by A. H. BLAKE. Herbert Jenkins, 1930.

Regional Architecture of the West of England, by RICHARDSON & Gill. Ernest Benn, Ltd., 1924.

The Eighteenth Century in London, by E. BERESFORD CHANCELLOR. Batsford, 1920.

London in the Eighteenth Century, by SIR WALTER BESANT. A. & C. Black, 1925.

Houses of the Wren and Early Georgian Periods, by SMALL and GOODRIDGE. Architectural Press, 1928.

The English Home from Charles II to George IV, by J. ALFRED GOTCH. Batsford, 1918.

London: the Unique City, by STEEN EILER RASMUSSEN. Jonathan Cape, 1937.

INDEX

(Figures in italics denote illustrations)

Ackerman's Repository, 141
Adam, Robert and James, 124-5, 128
Adelphi, The, 126
Albury House, Surrey, 87
Aldermaston House, 85
Althorp House, 101, 102
Anderson, Bertram, 66
Anglo-Saxon building, 22-8, *24, 29*
Aniline dyes, effect on colouring, 152
Antiques, Edwardian craze for, 157
Architect, function of, 10-12
Art nouveau, see "New Art" movement

Back-to-back houses, 132
Balconies, 128, 137
Bamboo furniture, 152
Banqueting Hall, Whitehall, 75, 98
Barnsley, Sidney, 159
Barry, Sir Charles, 134
Basements, 130, 146, 151
Bath, city of, 85, 95, 112
Beckford, William, 133
Beds, Roman, 17; Saxon, *27*, 30; Mediaeval, 33, 44; 16th century, 58; Elizabethan, 67, *71*; 18th century, 117; 19th century, 141; Victorian, 150
Bed hangings, 117, 141
Bedroom furniture, Victorian, 150
Bede, the Venerable, *quoted*, 23
Bell, Henry, architect, 100
Benches, Elizabethan, 67
Berkeley Square, 106
Black Death, the, 41, 45
Blenheim Palace, 111
"Blind" windows, 108
Bloomsbury Square, 106
Boat building, relation to Saxon architecture, 23, 25, 27, 28
Bond, English and Flemish, 54
Book cases, 116, 148
Bolsover, Thomas, 117
Bow windows, 128, 137
Braintree silk industry, 129
Brick making, Roman, 18
Brick work, Mediaeval, 37; Tudor, 54; 17th century, 78, 93, 96; 18th century, 112, 124; machine made, 132
Bricks, standardisation of, 78
Brighton, Pavilion at, 136, 137
Broad Hinton, 85
Brown, "Capability", 120
Bureaux, 116
Burlington, Earl of, 112, 116
Bushey Park, chestnut avenue at, 106

Cabinet makers, the great, 121-3
Cabriole legs introduced, 107
Caerleon, description of, 19, 21
Cambrensis, Giraldus, *quoted*, 19
Camden, William. *cited*, 70
"Camera" in Norman farmhouses, 37
Candles, Mediaeval, 40, 44; Saxon, 30
Candelabra, late 17th century, 95, *105*; 18th century, 117, 130
Candlesticks, Elizabethan, 67; early 18th century, *105*, 117; late 18th century, 130
Carpets, 79, 149
Cast iron introduced, 137
Castle, the Norman, 31-7, *32*
Castle Howard, Yorkshire, 111
Caversham House, 85
Celtic dwellings, 13
Cipriani, 129
Chadwick, Edwin, 140
Chairs, Mediaeval, 43; 16th century, 57, 58, *60*; Elizabethan, 66, 67; later 17th century, 78, 87, 88; Queen Anne, 107, 108; Windsor or stick-back, 109; 18th century, 116; Victorian, 148
Chambers, Sir William, 120
Chandeliers, crystal, 130; Elizabethan, 67-8
Charles II, 90, 93; *quoted*, 9
Chelsea Water Company, 131
Chests, Mediaeval, 33, *35*, 47; Tudor, 55, 57, *60*; Elizabethan, 65; late 17th century, 87
Chimneys, 88, 89, 91, 124; tax on, 91
Chimney corner, 89
Chimney pieces, 78, 128, 129
Chimney pots, 124, 137
China cabinets, 114
China, importations from, 95, 114
Chinese taste, furniture in the, 120, 126
Chippendale, Thomas, 121-2, 126
Chipping Campden, Glos., 49, *82, 142*
Chute, John, 127
Clap boarding, *see* Weather boarding
Clapham Park, 155
Classic revival, 126, 136
Climate, influence on building, 9-10, 162
Clocks, 87, 103, *104, 115*
Clock-makers, famous English, 103
Cobbett, William, 95, 96, 134, 136
Coke, in 17th century, 89
Coke, Sir Edward, *quoted* 73
Coggeshall Abbey, Essex, 37
Communal feeding, in mediaeval times, 40

Concrete houses, 162
Cooking utensils, Roman, 17; Saxon, 30;
  Mediaeval, 37, 44, 45; Elizabethan,
  70, 80; 18th century, 118, 130;
  Victorian, 151; see also Kitchens
Cooks, foreign, 69, 70
Cookshops, Mediaeval, 46, 47, 49
Cottages, 32, facing p. 32, 37, 38, 54, 59,
  64, 65, 81, 88, 92, 96, 102, 104, 109,
  110, 123, 133
Cottage ornée, the, 140, 148
Couches, 17, 141
Country houses: Roman, 16–7; Mediaeval,
  37; late Mediaeval, 41–4; Tudor, 53,
  54, 55; Elizabethan, 63, 64; Inigo
  Jones, 74–6, facing p. 80; Restoration
  period, 92–6; smaller type, 100;
  great house of 18th century, 101,
  102; late 18th century, 120–1, 130;
  early 19th century, 136; William
  Morris's, 151; 20th century types,
  158, 158, 159, 161
Crane, Sir Francis, 80
Croxdale, Durham, manor house, 66, 67
Crucks, system of building on, 27, 28
Cubitt, Thomas, 155
Cupboards: Corner, 116; Court, 67, 78;
  Hanging, 116
Curtains, 114, 141

"Dagswain" coverlets, 44, 58
Day beds, 17th century, 94
Director, Chippendale's, quoted 121, 122
Dog-legged stairs, 99, 100, 114
"Domus" in Norman farm buildings, 37
Drains, see Sanitation
Dressers, kitchen, 80
Dutch influence, 87, 107

Early English architecture, 35
Eglintoun Castle tournament (1839), 134
Electricity, 157, 158
Elizabeth, proclamation against over-
  crowding, 70–2
Embroidery, English, 26
Empire furniture, 141
Estate planning, 92, 106
Etruria, Wedgwood works at, 129, 130
Evans, Abel, quoted 112
Evelyn, Captain George, 87
Evelyn, John, Diary, quoted 83, 85, 86, 87,
  88, 100, 101, 102; on smoke abate-
  ment, 90, 91

Farmhouses, Mediaeval, 37, 44, 45; in 16th
  century, 55, 57, 58
"Farthingale" chair, 67
Fitz Ailwyne, mayor, 40
Fires, great, in London, 39, 46, 90, 91
Firebacks, 80
Fire dogs, 56, 68, 80
Fire grates, 80, 117

Fireplaces, Mediaeval, 40, 44, 49; Eliza-
  bethan, 68; see also Heating
Fitzroy Square, 126
Fitzstephen, William, quoted 39
Fladbury, Worcs., 86
Flats, 146
Flemish influence, 37
"Follies", architectural, 111, 121
Fonthill Abbey, 133
Food, Elizabethan, 69, 70
Forks, introduction of, 67
Four-poster beds, 58, 117
French windows, 137
"Functional" architecture, 162

Gardens, 53, 63, 85, 120, 143, 154
Garden City development, 155–6, 160
Garderobes, Mediaeval, 32, 33
Gas cooking and heating apparatus, 158
Gas fittings, 150, 151
Gas lighting introduced, 139, 140
Gesso work, 117
Gibbon, Edward, 153
Gimson, Ernest, 159
Glanvill, Sir John, 85
Gothic revival, 133, 134, 144, 145
"Gothic" taste, 126, 127, 133
Grandfather clocks, 103, 115
Grate, evolution of, 80, 117
Gray, Thomas, quoted 70
Grosvenor Square, 106

Half-timbered houses, 53, 82
Hall in Saxon dwellings, 25, 26; in Nor-
  man castles, 32, 36; later Mediaeval,
  42, 43, 45
Ham House, Petersham, 75
Hampstead Garden Suburb, 160
Hampton Court Palace, 53, 54, 98, 104
Harrison, William, quoted 56, 58, 64, 65,
  69, 70
Harrington, Sir John, 69
Hatfield, "The Eight Bells", facing p. 144
Hatton Garden, 80
"Headers" in brickwork, 54
Heal, Sir Ambrose, 159
Heating, of Roman houses, 17, 18; of
  Saxon, 25; Mediaeval, 32, 40
Heating, steam, 157
Hedingham Castle, fireplace at, 32
Hemans, Felicia, quoted, 133
Herbs, sweet, use of, 47, 69
Highwayman, Evelyn's experience of, 85
Holkham Hall, Norfolk, 116
Horse Guards Parade, 116
Hot water bottles, 150
Hot water supply, 150
Howard, Ebenezer, 155, 160
Huguenot craftsmen, 98
Hypocaust, method of heating, 17, 18

Industrial Revolution, effect on towns,
  132, 142–3

Inlay, definition of, 107
Iron working, Sussex, 58
Iron work, ornamental, 113, 128, 137
Italian influence, 51, 62, 74
Interiors, Roman, 16, 17, *20*; Saxon, 25,
    26, *27*; Mediaeval, 32, 33, 34, 35, 36,
    42, 43, 44; Tudor, *52*, 57, 58, 59;
    Elizabethan, 65–9; Early Stuart, 78–
    80; late 17th century, 87–8; early
    18th century, 103–4; mid-18th cen-
    tury, 114, 116, 117; late 18th century,
    124, *125*; Victorian, *147*, 148, 149,
    150, *facing p. 152*

Japanese influence, 152
Jellicoe, G. A., *facing p. 162*
"Jerry building", Mediaeval, 47; 19th
    century, 132, 138, 139; 20th century,
    160, 161
Johnson, Dr. Samuel, 100
Jonson, Ben, *The Devil is an Ass, quoted,*
    67; masques, 74; *The Staple of News,*
    quoted, 80
Jones, Inigo, 74–8, 87, 88, 90

Kauffman, Angelica, 129
Kent, William, 116, 120
Kensington Palace, 116
Kew, pagoda at, 120
King's Lynn, Norfolk, 100
Kingsley, Charles, *quoted,* 142
Kipling, Rudyard, *cited,* 19, 28
Kirby Hall, Northants., 74
Kitchens, Roman, 17; Saxon, 30; Medi-
    aeval, 37, 44; Elizabethan, 69, 70;
    late 17th century, 80; 18th century,
    117–8, 130; 19th century improve-
    ments, 139; Victorian, 151; early 20th
    century, 158
Kitchen dressers, 80
Kitchen range introduced, 80; improved,
    139

Lambeth Waterworks, 131
Lamps, *105, 122,* 139
Landscape gardening, 120
Langland, William, 43, 46
Langley Castle, Northumberland, garde-
    robe, 33
Lavenham, Suffolk, 49
Lantern clocks, 87, 103
Latten, 67
Le Corbusier, 162
Leech, John, 150
Lees Court, Faversham, 75
Leicester, Evelyn on, 88
Leicester Square, 106
Lighting of houses, early Mediaeval, 30;
    late Mediaeval, 44; Tudor, 67–8;
    18th century, 117, 130; Gas, 139, 140,
    158; electric, 158
Lindisfarne, Saxon church at, 23
"Linen-fold" pattern, 55, *60*

Link-holders, 113
Locksmith's work, 85
London in Roman times, 21; in Saxon
    times, 23, 29; in Mediaeval times,
    38–40, 46, 47; in Elizabethan times,
    70–2, *facing p. 72*; in 17th century,
    82, 88, 90, 91, 92, 93, 94; *facing p. 96,*
    100, 106; 18th century, 106, 112, 113,
    123, 125, 126; Adam's buildings in,
    124, 126; Nash's buildings in, 136,
    138; Gas lighting of streets, 139, 140
London: decay of street design in, 145;
    immense growth in Victorian times,
    153, 154; Norman Shaw's buildings,
    159
Long case clocks 103, *115*
Ludlow, *frontispiece*
Lutyens, Sir Edwin, 158

Machen, Arthur, *cited,* 19, 21
Mahogany furniture, 116
Manor houses, *see* Country houses
Market squares, *facing p. 112*
Marqueterie, definition of, 108
Materials, English building, 10, 16
Metal furniture, Roman, 17
Merchants' houses, in late Middle Ages,
    43, 46, 49, 50; Elizabethan, 62, 63
Mirabeau, Comte de, *quoted,* 119
Mirrors in decoration, 80, 108, 114
More, Thomas, *Utopia, quoted,* 51, 53
Morris, William, 151, 152, 156, 159,
    interior facing p. 152
Mortlake tapestries, 80
Mosaics, Roman, 16, 17
Mouldings applied to furniture, 116
Municipal Housing Schemes, 161, *facing p.*
    162

Nash, John, 136, 137, 138, *138*
Nevinson, Henry W., *quoted,* 153–4
"New Art" movement, 157
New Year celebrations at Caerleon, 19
Norman castles, 31, 32, 35; *facing pp. 32, 40*

Oak, 16th century use of, 59, 65
Orders, Roman, 14, *15*, 62, *79*
Ornament: 16th century, 55; Elizabethan,
    61–2; Jacobean, 73; 17th century, 88;
    Chinese, 126; Adam, 129; Regency,
    137; Victorian, 148–9
Overcrowding in Elizabethan times, 71;
    in late 17th century, 88; 18th
    century, 100; 19th century, 132

Painted decoration, 16, 34, 95, 128, 129
Palladio's designs published, 112
Pall Mall, 106
Panelled rooms, *52*, 55, 79, *84*, 114
Papier-maché furniture, 149
Parks, laying out of, 106, 120
Park Lane, 123
Parliament, Houses of, 134

Peasants, housing of, in Roman times, 18; Saxon, 32; Mediaeval, 37, 38; Tudor, 54, 59; *see also* Cottages
Penshurst Place, 43
Pepys, Samuel, *cited*, 91, 92, 94, 95
Perpendicular architecture, 53
Pergolesi, 129
Pewter, Elizabethan, 67
Pillows, Mediaeval, 44, 58
Plasterwork, exterior, 46, 47, 110; interior, 55, 63, 68, 128
Plate, Elizabethan, 67; 18th century, 117
Pope, Alexander, *quoted*, 110, 111, 112, 118
Porcelain, 18th century, 129, 130
Portland Place, 126
Portland stone, 94
Postman, The, Nov. 18th, 1701, *quoted*, 118
Povey, Mr., house described, 95
Privacy, development of, 32, 35
Public Health Legislation, 140
Pugin, A. W., 134

Queen Anne furniture, 107–9
Queen Anne revival, 159
Queen's Square, Bloomsbury, 113
"Queen's Ware", Wedgwood's, 129

Raynham Hall, Norfolk, 75, 98
Red Lion Square, Holborn, 106
Regency building, 136, 137, *et seq.*, *facing pp. 128, 136, 138*
Regency furniture, 141
Regent's Park, 136, *138*
Ribbon development, 160
Richmond, Yorks., cottages at, *88*
Robertson, Howard, *quoted*, 11, 12
Ruins, 18th century taste for, 121, 126
Rushes, on floor, 29, 79
Ruskin, John, 144, 145, 148
Russell, Gordon, 159

St. Ives, cottages at, *102*
St. James's Square, 106
St. Paul's Cathedral, 70
St. Paul's, manors of, 37
Salisbury, Evelyn on, 86, 87
Sanitation, Roman, 14; Saxon, 26; Mediaeval, 32, 33, 39; Elizabethan, 60, 69; 17th century, 91; 18th century, 118, 130; 19th century improvements, 140
Sash windows, 76, 98, *99*
Satinwood furniture, 129
Scott, Sir Walter, 133, 134
Seaton Delaval, Northumberland, 111
Sedgefield, Durham, 16th century rectory, 66
Serfs, *see* Peasants
Servants' quarters, 63, 101, 139, 146
Settles, Elizabethan, 67

Shaw, Norman, 159
Sheets, 44, 58
Sheffield Plate, 117
Sheraton, Thomas, 121
Sideboards, 121, 149
Silchester collection of Roman antiquities, 17
Slums, mediaeval, 47, 49; Tudor, 59; 19th century, 132, 142–3; clearance schemes, 161
Smoke nuisance, 89, 90, 91, 124, 142, 143
Smoker's set, *131*
Soho Square, 106
Solar, mediaeval, 32, 43
Somerset House, 120
Southampton Row, 113
Spanish influence, 66, 67
Spitalfields silk, 114, 129
Squares, the London, 106, 113
Stairs, development of, 99, 100, 114
Standardisation of bricks, 78
Stick-back chairs, 109
Stools, buffet, 67; joint or coffin, 67
Stow, *Annales*, *quoted*, 81–2
Stratford Place, Oxford Street, 126
"Strawberry Hill" Gothic, 126, 127, 128
Streets, Mediaeval, 47, *48*, 49; 16th century, 59, 70, *facing p. 72*; 17th century, 82, *facing p. 96*, 100, 106; 18th century, 112, 113, 124, 126, *facing 128, 138*; decay of design, 145
Stucco, 124, 136
Suburb, the Victorian, 153, 154, 155; the Edwardian, 156; Modern, 160–1
Surtees, R. S., *quoted*, 148, 150
Sycamore introduced, 59

Tables, 66, 78, 117
Tallboys, 116
Tapestry in decoration, 33, 80
Tax on chimneys, 91; on windows, 99, 108, 146; on bricks, 124
Tea, introduction of, 95; Cobbett on, 134
Tea tables, 117
"Teapot Hall", Scrivelsby, Lincs., 28
Tenement houses, 146
Thatching, 22, 40, 46
Thorne, Robert, of Bristol, *quoted*, 61
Thorpe, John, 74, 75, 76
Tile-hung houses, *75*, 110
Timber, early use of, 10, 25, 27, 28; growing shortage of, 81
Timber-framed houses, 47, *48*
Tompion, Thomas, 103
Town houses, Roman, 19, 21; Mediaeval, 38, 39, 40, 46, 47, 48, 49; Tudor, 50, 59, 60; Elizabethan, *68*, 70; 17th century, *80*, 93, 94, 95, 100, 103; 18th century, *112*, 113, 117, 124, 128, 132; Regency, 136, *facing p. 136*, *138*; Victorian, 145–6
Trees, importation of, 21, 106, 120

Upholstery, introduction of, 78; great use of in 18th century, 108, 116; 19th century, 141
Upton, The Red House, 151

Van der Velde's *Art nouveau*, 157
Vanbrugh, Sir John, 111–2
Veneèring, 108
Verandahs, 128, 137
Vermuyden, Cornelius, 87
Verulamium, 27
Villa, the Roman, 14, 16, 17, *20*
Village craftsmen, 96, 109, 121, 122
Vine pattern, 55
Vitruvius, *quoted*, 11, 16
Voysey, C. F. A., 158
Vyne, The, 127

Wainscotting, *see* Panelled rooms
Wall papers, 114, 141, 149
Walnut furniture, 103, 107
Walpole, Horace, 126, 127
Water-closets, 69, 131, 140
Water supply, London, 39, 118, 131
Watering-places, development of, *facing p. 128*, 136, *facing p. 136*
Weatherboarded houses, *109*, 110, 132

Webb, Philip, 151
Wedgwood, Josiah, 129–30
Wells, the London, 39
Wells, H. G., *quoted*, 153
Welwyn Garden City, 160
Whitehall Palace, 75
Wilton House, 75
Windows, Roman, 16; Saxon, *29*, *30*; Mediaeval, 35, 37, 38, 42; late Perpendicular, *52*, 53, 55; 16th century, *58*, 68; 17th century, 76, *77*; mullion and sash, 98, *99*; 18th century, 108, 128; early 19th century, 137; Victorian, 146
Window boxes, 146
Window draperies, 114, 141, 146
Window tax, 99, 108, 146
Windsor chairs, 109
Winter, Sir John, 89
Withdrawing room, *see* Solar
Woodwork, Mediaeval, 47
Wood, John, father and son, 112
"Wool" towns, 49
Wotton, Sir Henry, 73
Wren, Sir Christopher, 85, 90, 92, 104
Wyatt, James, 133

Zucchi, 129